GLOVES GONE BY

Heavyweight Boxers from the Glorious Era 1960 to 1980

James Amato

authorHOUSE®

AuthorHouse™
1663 Liberty Drive
Bloomington, IN 47403
www.authorhouse.com
Phone: 1 (800) 839-8640

Foreword by Jerry Fitch
Edited by Deborah Kause and Michael Stolarczyk

Published by AuthorHouse 10/26/2017

ISBN: 978-1-5462-1412-0 (sc)
ISBN: 978-1-5462-1410-6 (hc)
ISBN: 978-1-5462-1411-3 (e)

Library of Congress Control Number: 2017916298

Print information available on the last page.

This book is printed on acid-free paper.

DEDICATION

This book is dedicated to my children Michael,
Angelene, Anthony and James.

They are my legacy.

James Amato

FOREWORD

Although I did not meet Jim Amato in person until a few years ago, I have corresponded with him for a long time. I was well aware of him years before meeting him, and I learned about his involvement with various boxing organizations both in Ohio and nationally. Over the years I read his boxing stories that appeared in several publications and websites, including Boxing World, which both of us have a long history with. Not only could I feel his passion for boxing, but I also realized he knew what he was talking about.

Jim has lived in Ashland, Ohio for many years but is a former Clevelander and a die-hard Cleveland sports fan, but more than that, he has been an avid boxing fan for most of his life, probably even before he found out that his Great Uncle Joe Amato had been a boxer in the 1920s.

This is Jim's first effort at writing a book, and he shows his passion for the contenders he writes about just as he has in many of his other boxing endeavors. The stories are from his collection of prose that he has written over many years. Now for the first time you can read some of his best writing efforts all in one place.

I am sure you will enjoy them as much as I have.

Jerry Fitch

Cleveland Boxing Author/ Historian

November 2016

Jerry Fitch is "The Dean of Cleveland Boxing Writers"
who has authored five outstanding books.

"Cleveland's Greatest Fighters", "James Louis Bivins, The Man Who
Would Be Champion", "50 Years of Fights And Friends", "Johnny Risko,
The Cleveland Rubberman", and his latest book, "My Favorite Fights".

For information on Jerry's books, you can contact
him at jerryfitch1946@gmail.com

A TRIBUTE TO SAL MARINO

In 1993 I contacted a man named Jim Borgen answering an ad in a magazine. He was a boxing memorabilia collector, and I was looking for boxing books. After our conversation, Jim invited me to a sports bar in the Youngstown area to watch the live broadcast of the Bowe – Holyfield rematch, (The Fan Man fight). We have been friends ever since. In the early years of our friendship, Jim often mentioned Sal Marino. Sal was a respected and influential man in the Youngstown boxing area. It would be over five years before I would actually meet Sal. We met at a boxing banquet outside of Youngstown in 1999. We seemed to hit it off, and over the years, Sal took me under his wing. Sal and Jim became mentors to me. Over the next decade I learned so much about the rich boxing history of the Youngstown area from these two men. I learned about Tony Janiro and Sonny Horne, about Tommy Bell and Lenny "Boom Boom" Mancini (Ray's Dad), and of course Harry Arroyo, Greg Richardson, Ray Mancini, Jeff Lampkin and a young Kelly Pavlik.

Sal was President and co-founder of the Trumbull County (Ohio) Legends of Leather Boxing Club. Although he loved boxing, he was also well versed in other sports such as football and baseball. At times he had his own newspaper column and radio sports talk show. He was a charming and personable man with a quick wit. He was also a very caring individual. When I had some serious health problems a few years back, Sal and Jim stayed in close contact. Sal even sent me a blessed rosary. That sure meant a lot to me.

In 2006 Sal nominated me for the Legends of Leather Hall Of Fame. I was inducted later that year. The trophy and ring I received are among my prize possessions. Sal passed away late last year after a brave battle with cancer. Although I only knew Sal for a decade or so, he had a fatherly type influence on me. I know he is greatly missed by his family and friends who are trying to keep the Legends of Leather going. I am honored to say he was my friend. Rest in peace Sal.

PART ONE

THE PERCEPTION

It is not fun growing old. I am a product of my past, a victim of my era, so to speak. I constantly bump heads with the young fans of today. They glorify Hopkins, Manny, Mayweather and the Klitschko brothers. Even from a decade or so before, it's all about Holyfield, Whitaker and a guy named Mike Tyson. They are all great fighters in their own right. Then you can go back a little farther. Now we're talking Holmes, Duran, Hagler, Leonard, Hearns, Pryor, Michael Spinks and Benitez. How about Julio Cesar Chavez, Edwin Rosario and the great Salvador Sanchez? These are all great names and outstanding fighters.

I honestly feel I was very fortunate to grow up in a period of some truly great fighters. Boxers... champions who dominated their respective divisions. This isn't about Ali and Frazier. The mark they left on boxing is stamped for eternity. No, this is about dominant champions like Bob Foster, Dick Tiger, Emile Griffith, Carlos Monzon, Jose Napoles, Antonio Cervantes, Roberto Duran, Carlos Ortiz, Flash Elorde, Alexis Arguello, Vincente Saldivar, Eder Jofre, Fighting Harada, Ruben Olivares, Carlos Zarate, Pascual Perez and Miguel Canto.

Then you have boxers, who in today's state of fragmented titles, would have surely won a piece of the pie. Tough men like Jerry Quarry, Yaqui Lopez, Bennie Briscoe, Hedgemon Lewis, Ernie "Red" Lopez, Armando Muniz, Clyde Gray and Ray Lampkin, just to mention a few.

Yes, I admit that I live in the past, but these boxers, and so many others from that era, continue to stir up great fistic memories. We will never know for sure if Hopkins could have defeated Monzon or Hagler. We'll never know if Bob Foster could have defeated Michael Spinks or Roy Jones Jr. I just don't want to let the greatness of the fistic heroes I grew up with be forgotten. Just as I hope the fistic heroes of today will be remembered thirty years down the road.

JOE ALEXANDER

He had less than twenty professional fights, but for anyone who followed the heavyweight division in the 1970's, they will never forget Joe Alexander. In his twelve victories he scored ten knockouts. This guy could bang! Joe was a New Yorker turned pro in 1968. He was short for a heavyweight at 5'9". In his second bout, Alexander suffered a one round knockout defeat. Hey, I didn't say he had Jake LaMotta's chin.

In 1969 filling in as a substitute, he was halted by the capable Hal Carroll. No shame in that defeat since Carroll was a ranked fighter. Joe came back in 1972, and in 1973, Joe outscored rugged veteran Leroy Caldwell. Two months later he shook up the heavyweight division with a shocking one round blitz of Venezuela's world ranked contender Jose Luis Garcia. In 1974 he was put in as a "tune up" for the highly ranked Jerry Quarry. Joe hadn't read the script. Jerry was as tough as they come, and he had a great chin. In the first round though, Joe floored Jerry, and Quarry was lucky to get up and survive the round. Jerry showed his pluck in round two as he gathered himself to halt Joe. Nevertheless, Alexander had made a statement.

Alexander would win three straight by one round knockouts. He followed that with a two round victory. Then he outscored tough journeyman G.G. Maldonado. Joe then went to Las Vegas where he dropped a ten rounder to talented Kevin Issac. Alexander would lose decisions in 1979 and 1981 and retire. His final ledger was 12-7. He may not have been a top contender, but he was a very dangerous man.

OSCAR BONAVENA

When Oscar Bonavena of Argentina started his professional career in 1964, he met tough opponents like Tom McNeely and Dick Wipperman. In his first bout in 1965, he was overmatched and defeated by veteran contender Zora Folley. Oscar then left New York and returned to Argentina. He defeated Gregorio Peralta and American import Billy Daniels. When he returned to New York in 1966, he outpointed the equally rugged George Chuvalo.

Oscar was then matched with 1964 Olympic Gold Medal winner Joe Frazier. The fight was classic. Oscar had Joe down twice, but Frazier came back to win a close decision. In 1967 Oscar was entered in the World Boxing Association eight man elimination tourney to determine the defrocked Muhammad Ali's successor. In his first match, Oscar traveled to Germany and trounced southpaw Karl Mildenberger. In his next bout, Bonavena was floored twice and soundly beaten by the eventual tourney winner Jimmy Ellis. Oscar regrouped in 1968 beating Folley in a rematch and also the respected Leotis Martin. He was then matched again with Joe Frazier for the New York State version of the heavyweight crown. Oscar fell behind early, but he came back strong only to drop the fifteen round verdict.

Bonavena would remain a mainstay in the talent rich rankings until the untimely end of his career. Two years after his loss to Frazier, Oscar would face Muhammad Ali who had returned from exile. It would be one of the most grueling fights of Ali's career. The "Greatest" came out on top stopping a dead game but exhausted Oscar in the fifteenth and final round.

In 1971 Bonavena won by disqualification over Al "Blue" Lewis. In 1972 he met former world champion Floyd Patterson. Oscar lost a very debatable decision. Two years later Ron Lyle defeated Bonavena. This loss pretty much pushed Oscar out of the title picture. Bonavena was still a rated contender when on May 22, 1976, he was shot and killed at a brothel in Las Vegas.

JOE BUGNER

Joe Bugner won (69-13-1, 41 KO's) and may well be one of the most underrated heavyweights over the last forty years. His record speaks for itself. Really you say…

Before you laugh look at the facts. Joe was born in 1950 and turned pro in 1967. He was still fighting well into the 90's. His record is a who's who of the heavyweights of that era. He went the distance with Muhammad Ali twice. His second encounter was in a losing effort for the championship. In all, he traveled 27 rounds with the "Greatest". He also went 12 rugged rounds with Joe Frazier, losing a close verdict. Bugner did win decision victories over title claimants Jimmy Ellis and Greg Page. Past his prime, he was halted by future titleholder Frank Bruno.

During his prime he defeated the best that England and the rest of Europe could offer. He met world title challengers like Henry Cooper, Brian London, Manuel Ramos, Ron Lyle, Earnie Shavers, Chuck Wepner, Marvis Frazier, Steffen Tangstad, James Tillis, David Bey and Richard Dunn. He also met several other respectable big men such as Mac Foster, Jose Luis Garcia, Larry Middleton, Eduardo Corletti, Jurgen Blin, Jack Bodell and Jack O'Halloran.

Bugner, who was born in Hungary, boxed out of England and later fought out of Australia. He was tall and well proportioned. He was a smart boxer with a good left jab. He was very mobile for a man his size and he had a pretty fair right cross. He also had a solid chin.

Jerry Quarry was a terrific fighter, but Bugner fared much better against Ali and Frazier than Jerry did. George Chuvalo also went 27 rounds with Ali. He also went the full route with Ellis, Floyd

Patterson and Ernie Terrell. Still he was butchered by Frazier and George Foreman.

Gerry Cooney could bang, but I don't believe he ever had the chance to truly mature as a fighter. Tommy Morrison had a good punch and decent skills but no chin. Duane Bobick was a solid puncher, but slow and not very durable. Chuck Wepner was awkward and as game as they come, but he could be easily out boxed. Henry Cooper had a great left hook, but he cut easy, and his chin was shaky. Boone Kirkman could punch, but he had no defense. Randy Neuman was a good boxer but a light hitter. Karl Mildenberger was troublesome from his southpaw stance but little else. Ron Stander and Scott LeDoux, like Wepner, were game to core. If courage alone won titles, they would have been champs.

THE RISE AND NEVER FALL OF GEORGE CHUVALO

For most of the 1960's and part of the early 1970's Canadian George Chuvalo was a mainstay in the talent rich heavyweight ratings. RING Magazine founder Nat Fleischer called George one of the most durable fighters he had ever seen. In his long distinguished career the rock jawed Chuvalo was NEVER off his feet. Amazing seeing the competition he faced. For the sake of space let's start looking at George's career from 1965 on.

Chuvalo's 1965 bout with ex-world champion Floyd Patterson was one of the year's best action fights. George never stopped coming forward as he landed clubbing rights to Floyd's head and terrific lefts to his body. Still Floyd showed a heart that everyone doubted he had. He absorbed Chuvalo's fury and used his outstanding hand speed to win a popular decision over George. Although George lost, his courage impressed the crowd. Despite the losing effort, Chuvalo was matched with World Boxing Association titleholder Ernie Terrell. When Ali met Sonny Liston in their rematch, the W.B.A. stripped Ali and recognized the winner of a Terrell-Eddie Machen bout. Terrell captured a boring verdict and the "vacant" crown. Against Chuvalo, the 6'7" Terrell used a long jab and a grab and clutch style to outscore George over fifteen rounds.

The roller coaster career of Chuvalo continued into 1966. George traveled to London and was upset by Argentina's Eduardo Corletti in ten rounds. The loss appeared to have pushed George out of the title picture. Instead, he benefited by being in the right place at the right time. When a proposed Ali-Terrell fight fell through, Ali agreed to come to Toronto and defend against George. Although the bout was entertaining, it was also one sided. Try as he might, George was unable to reach the fleet-footed Ali. For all his efforts, Chuvalo received numerous jabs, hooks, uppercuts and crosses from a prime Ali. Even in losing, George received the respect of the public for his gaminess. Later in the year, Chuvalo met fellow brawler Oscar Bonevena of Argentina. What looked to be a great match up between the two sluggers turned out to be a dud. Oscar "finessed" George to win a ten round decision.

George got back on track in 1967. Two kayo victories over Willi Besmanoff led to Chuvalo being matched with the streaking Joe Frazier. "Smokin" Joe had won the 1964 Olympic Gold Medal and was undefeated as a pro. George was to be his toughest match to date. Frazier was at his best in this battle as he ravaged George throughout with his famous left hook. To his credit, George gamely refused to fall, but the referee saved him in round four. Again just as it appeared that George's tenure as a top contender was over, Chuvalo got one more chance. An impressive upset kayo win over highly regarded Mexican Manuel Ramos put him back in the rankings. His success was short lived. In 1969 he met huge Buster Mathis. Buster's only loss had been to Frazier, and he needed to win to set up a rematch with Joe or a shot at the W.B.A. titleholder Jimmy Ellis. Mathis, who was a fine boxer for a big man, gave George a boxing lesson over twelve rounds. George closed out 1969 in a "White Hope" battle versus popular but erratic Jerry Quarry. For six rounds, the Irishman outboxed Chuvalo, who was cut and bleeding. Jerry looked to be on his way to a comfortable point win or even a TKO. In round seven George went for broke and clubbed Jerry to the canvas. Quarry was listening to the referee's count on one knee, but at "10" he failed to rise. Jerry quickly jumped up and claimed he had lost track of the count, but his protesting fell on deaf ears, and Chuvalo's kayo victory had him back in the top ten.

The win over Quarry landed George another bout with an Olympic hero. George Foreman had won the Gold Medal in 1968, and he was climbing quickly up the professional ladder. A win over Chuvalo would look nice on his record. The bigger, stronger Foreman was in control from the start. He pummeled Chuvalo at will, and in the third round, he sent Chuvalo reeling across the ring. Only the ropes prevented a knockdown. Still Chuvalo kept his feet but was defenseless against Foreman's follow up barrage, and the referee stepped in. In 1971 Chuvalo dropped a ten round duke to ex-champion Jimmy Ellis. George did manage a points win over still dangerous ex-contender Cleveland Williams. In 1972 Chuvalo got yet another opportunity as he again faced Muhammad Ali. Ali had lost to Frazier in 1971's "Battle of the Century", and now he was taking on all comers while awaiting a rematch with Joe. Although George gave a respectable showing, the great Ali again outclassed him.

From this point on, George slowly faded from the picture. He hung around a few more years dominating the Canadian heavyweight scene, but his days as a world class contender were over. Still after absorbing the punches of Ali, Frazier, Foreman, Quarry, Patterson and Ellis, he stood tall with his feet planted firmly on the ground. He wouldn't have it any other way.

HENRY CLARK

There was many who thought he was going to be the next Cassius Clay/ Muhammad Ali. He was a tall, smooth boxing heavyweight with a world of potential. His professional career began in 1964, and before long he was mixing it up with some of the best fighters in the world. How's this for starters? His pro debut was a four round decision loss to the rugged Joey Orbillo!

Less than two months later he pounded out a ten round verdict over future title challenger Manuel Ramos. The following year he whipped tough trial horse George "Scrap Iron" Johnson. In 1966 he fought a No Decision bout with Amos "Big Train" Lincoln, and he lost a decision to highly regarded Zora Folley. The year 1967 saw Henry establish himself as a force in the heavyweight division by winning on points over Bill McMurray, Steve Grant on two occasions, Fred Lewis, Eddie Machen and Roger Rischer.

Henry opened 1968 by defeating the clever Leotis Martin. This led Henry into a major bout against come backing ex-heavyweight king Sonny Liston. This was Sonny's first major step on his comeback trail, and he passed with flying colors. Sonny pummeled a game, but overmatched Clark in scoring a seventh round stoppage.

The year 1969 had mixed results. Henry drew with Brian London and kayoed Bob Stallings. He then lost on points to "Florida" Al Jones and Jeff "Candy Slim" Merritt. In 1970 his best win was a points call over Jimmy "The King" Fletcher. In 1972 Henry won and lost to Jack "The Giant" O'Halloran. He was then stopped in nine rounds by an up and coming Ken Norton on the Muhammad Ali-Bob Foster undercard.

Henry came back to win three bouts in 1973, and then on March 4th, 1974, in a rematch, Henry blew out the now ranked Jeff Merritt in one round. Henry quickly followed with a decision win over faded ex-contender Mac Foster. Henry remained unbeaten through four more fights and was then matched with the dangerous Earnie Shavers in Paris, France.

Try as he might for the KO, Shavers was unable to stop the wily Clark and had to settle for a hard earned points win over Henry. They met again six months later on the undercard of Ali-Norton III. This time Henry was overwhelmed by the murderous punching Shavers in two rounds.

Henry attempted to bounce back four months later but was defeated over ten by Howard "Kayo" Smith. Henry did not fight again for over two and a half years. When he did return, he was defeated in ten rounds by fringe contender Bernardo Mercado.

Henry's final tally was 32 wins, 12 losses and four draws. He scored seven knockouts, but he was only stopped on three occasions by Liston, Norton and Shavers, surely no shame there.

ROBERT CLEROUX

No doubt the most well-known modern day heavyweight from Canada is George Chuvalo. For a while Lennox Lewis claimed Canada as his home. Trevor Berbick made his mark as did Razor Ruddock. Still George is #1. People tend to forget that Chuvalo lost two out of three fights to his equally rugged countryman Robert Cleroux. "Big Bob" was once one fight away from a title shot. An untimely upset loss ended that dream.

Cleroux was born on February 23, 1938. He joined the punch for pay ranks in 1957 after winning the Montreal Golden Gloves title in 1956. At 6'1" and weighing over 200 pounds, he was a fairly big heavyweight in his era. He won twelve of his first thirteen contests. Only a draw with Eddie Vick stained his record. He beat Eddie in a return go. Vick would go on to fight the likes of Tommy "Hurricane" Jackson, Chuck Wepner, Jeff Merritt and Bob Foster twice during his career. Bob invaded New York's Madison Square Garden in 1959 and suffered his first loss, an eight round decision, to veteran Buddy Turman.

Cleroux would regroup to win nine in a row, including a decision over Willie Besmanoff and a five round kayo against Roy "Cut-N-Shoot" Harris. In 1960 he won a close and hard fought split decision over Chuvalo to capture the Canadian crown. Later in the year he would drop a twelve round verdict to George losing the title. In between those two battles, Bob halted Turman in two rounds to gain a measure of revenge.

1961 was a good year for Robert as he stopped Harold Carter, Harris again and the hard hitting Alex Miteff. He then won another split decision over Chuvalo to recapture the Canadian heavyweight championship. He defended that title by knockout over Cecil Gray and then stopped rugged George Logan in seven. Then Bob hit a rough patch dropping ten rounders to the highly rated Zora Folley and tough Mike DeJohn. He then won a close points call against Tom McNeely. Cleroux followed that with four straight knockout victories and was again paired with the clever Folley. Zora clearly out boxed Cleroux, and Bob stepped away from the ring for five years.

When Cleroux returned in 1968, he quickly won five straight bouts. He then outduked the still dangerous Cleveland Williams to re-establish himself as a contender for world honors. In 1969 he whipped Charlie Chase twice and Bob Felstein. It was now rumored that Bob was going to challenge Jimmy Ellis for the World Boxing Association version of the heavyweight title. In July he met Billy Joiner in a tune up bout. Joiner, a former Ohio standout amateur boxer and capable professional fighter, upset the apple cart by winning a ten round split decision. With this defeat Cleroux's hopes for a title shot were dashed, and he retired for good.

In 55 fights Bob posted a very respectable 48-6-1 record. He won 38 by knockout, and he was never stopped.

SIR HENRY COOPER

He came from a fighting family and by the time his boxing career ended in 1971, he was the most beloved British boxer of all time. Only once did he challenge for the World's title, but he dominated the British heavyweight scene for over fifteen years. His popularity soared even more after retirement, and eventually the Queen of England knighted him. Sir Henry Cooper was more than just a British fighter. He was a fine example of what British boxing is all about.

Henry's professional career started in September of 1954, and he proceeded to win his first nine fights including an eight round points win over Joe Bygraves. In Henry's tenth bout he lost the first of many bouts due to an eye cut to Uber Bacilleri. He would later avenge that loss. The roller coaster career of Henry Cooper had now begun. He would drop a ten rounder to Joe Erskine and stop Brian London in one round. Then he would lose to Peter Bates in five rounds. 1955 was a rough year for Henry as Bygraves kayoed him for the British Empire Commonwealth title. Future world champion Ingemar Johansson then bombed him out in a bout for the European championship. Joe Erskine then outscored him for the British title. Henry began to turn things around late in 1958 with a stoppage over Dick Richardson and a points win over respected American Zora Folley.

He finally won the British and Empire titles by a decision over Brian London in 1959. He halted Gawie de Klerk in an Empire defense and defended both titles by a fifth round stoppage of Joe Erskine. In 1960 Henry scored important decision victories of Roy "Cut-N-Shoot" Harris and Alex Mitiff. He again defended his titles by a fifth round stoppage of Erskine in March of 1961. On December 5, 1961, Henry suffered a major setback when Folley kayoed him in the second round of their rematch. He came back to again stop Erskine in 1962 and Dick Richardson in 1963 setting the stage for a match with the undefeated Olympian Cassius Clay. The facts of Cooper's first bout with Clay have been well documented with his left hook knocking Clay down at the end of round four. A torn glove supposedly gave Clay time to recover. Cassius then came back to cut and stop Henry in round five. Cooper came back after the defeat to Clay by beating Brian London again also winning the vacant European title in the process. Six months later he was stripped of the European title due to an injury. Henry would win five of his next seven bouts setting up a title shot and rematch against Clay (Muhammad Ali). The rematch was anti-climactic. Henry tried hard, but Ali's punches again ripped the tender skin above Cooper's eye forcing a stoppage. Four months later, ex-title holder Floyd Patterson felled Henry.

It was again time to rebuild. Henry went back to retaining his British and Empire titles defeating Jack Bodell and Billy Walker. He then regained the European title winning on a disqualification from Karl Mildenberger. In 1969 Henry was to be matched with World Boxing Association champion Jimmy Ellis. The fight fell through because the British Boxing Board refused to recognize it as a world title fight. In a huff, Henry gave up the British and Empire titles. Later Henry relinquished the European crown due to an injury. Again in 1970 the amazing Cooper came back to regain the British and Empire titles from Jack Bodell. Later he regained the European crown by stopping Jose Urtain. On March 16, 1971, Henry met upcoming Joe Bugner with all three titles at stake. After fifteen well contested rounds, Bugner was awarded a very close and controversial decision much to the dismay of Henry. Cooper never boxed again.

Cooper retired with a fine 40-14-1 record. He faced three world champions and five others who fought for the title.

JOHN "DINO" DENIS

In the talent laden heavyweight era of the 1970's...a few notable fighters have slipped through the cracks. One such fighter was Massachusetts native, John "Dino" Denis. He was as game as they come, and he battled some of the best of his era. Born in 1951, John turned professional in 1972. By 1976 he would run his record up to an impressive 28-0-1. Among the notables he defeated were Terry Daniels, Mike Boswell, Joe "King" Roman and the rugged Scott LeDoux. It all came crashing down in 1976 when Dino was slated on the comeback trail of George Foreman. Dino showed the heart of a lion but was finally overwhelmed by Foreman's power in round four.

In 1977 Dino dropped a decision to a talented big guy named Leroy Jones. Denis would then win seven in a row which would lead him to a 1979 match against the red hot Gerry Cooney. Dino just ended up becoming another notch in the gun as Big Gerry stopped him in round three. Dino then reeled off nine straight before a surprising KO loss to Donnie Long in 1982. The loss to Long pretty much put Denis out of the rankings. In 1983 Dino was halted by the under rated and effective Joe Bugner. John retired, but then in 1990, he had a two fight come back. He then retired for good. In all, John fought 52 contests. He ended up with a very respectable 45-5-2 record. He was a true "tough guy"!!!

TONY DOYLE

He came out of Salt Lake City with dreams of becoming heavyweight champion. He turned pro well before his twentieth birthday and met some of the best heavyweights of his day.

Tony Doyle was another in a long string of white, Irish contenders who would have an impact on the heavyweight ratings in the late 60's and early 70's.

Tony turned pro in 1963 and reeled off seven straight wins before meeting and losing to his nemesis James J. Woody via a ten round verdict. Two fights later he lost by a decision to another experienced boxer named Chuck Leslie.

The cycle of Tony's rollercoaster career had begun. He kayoed Archie Ray in his next fight, and again two fights later he drew with another up and coming Irishman named Jerry Quarry.

Three fights later he was outfought by the rugged Joey Orbillo. Tony traveled to Las Vegas and avenged his loss to Leslie, only to lose his next match to promising James Rosette.

On October 17th, 1967, Tony got a big break when he traveled to Philadelphia to meet the soaring 1964 Olympic gold medalist winner Joe Frazier. This was to be a stern test for Joe, but he walked right through Tony destroying him in two rounds.

Amazingly Doyle bounced back to win ten straight fights including victories over Jack O' Halloran and Amos "Big Train "Lincoln. He dropped a ten rounder to the formidable Manuel Ramos and then put together another seven fight win streak. Roberto Davila and Thad Spencer were among his victims.

1970 he lost back to back fights to James J. Woody that slowed his career. In 1971 Tony lost an important bout to Jimmy Ellis but came back to beat a faded Spencer again. He then lost a rematch to Jerry Quarry by decision.

In 1972 Tony lost to Larry Middleton and was kayoed by Joe Bugner. In 1973 Quarry ended his trilogy with Doyle scoring a smashing fourth round knockout. Howard "Kayo" Smith stopped Tony in 1974, and in 1975 he was outscored by Johnny Boudreaux.

On June 27, 1975, Tony was belted out in nine rounds by future champion Mike Weaver. In his career Doyle met three champions, Frazier, Ellis, and Weaver. He also met several top contenders of his time in Quarry, Spencer, Middleton, Bugner and Ramos. In addition he took on a lot of rough characters like Orbillo and O' Halloran, and for that he will be remembered.

JIMMY ELLIS

It's too bad that the cruiserweight division was not around in the 60's and 70's. Many fine boxers scaled under 200 pounds and gave creditable performances against bigger men. Doug Jones is an example as he came close to upsetting Cassius Clay in 1963. Doug had lost in 1962 to Harold Johnson for the light heavyweight title. In 1965 he lost to Ernie Terrell for WBA Heavyweight crown. Back then there was no middle ground. If you weighed over 175 pounds, you fought heavyweights, period.

Bob Foster, who was one of the greatest light heavyweights of all time, had trouble moving up to heavyweight. Jones, Terrell, and Zora Foley soundly beat him in heavyweight bouts. After winning the light heavyweight crown in 1968, he failed in attempts to beat Joe Frazier and Muhammad Ali. How would he have fared at 200 pounds?

I'm sure if you took all the top boxers who weighed between 175 pounds and 200 pounds since 1960, most experts would rate Holyfield number one. How would a 200 pound Holyfield have coped with Floyd Patterson's hand speed? How about Bob Foster's reach and devastating punch? Could he have beaten Jimmy Ellis? Before you laugh, take a look at Jimmy's record. He started as a middleweight in 1961, and through 1964, he lost five bouts to Holly Mims, Henry Hank, Rubin Carter, Don Fuller and George Benton, all top middleweight contenders. By the time he blasted out Johnny Persol in one round in 1967, he had grown into a heavyweight. He swept the WBA elimination tournament by beating Leotis Martin, Oscar Bonevena and Jerry Quarry. Jimmy twice had the iron jawed Bonevena on the canvas. Something Joe Frazier could not do in 25 rounds of fighting. When Ellis met Frazier in February of 1970 to unify the title, he weighed in over 200 pounds. He looked flabby and after a few rounds became sluggish. Joe took out a game but outgunned Ellis after four rounds.

The following year Jimmy met his longtime friend Muhammad Ali. Jimmy was in great shape at 189 pounds. His muscles were tight and he looked fit. Unfortunately, Ali was too big. He wore Jimmy down and stopped him in round twelve. I believe the Jimmy Ellis of the Ali fight could have given any 200 pounder since 1960 a run for their money, including Evander Holyfield. Ellis was a slick boxer with sharp reflexes. He had a good left hand and a sneaky right. He also had loads of courage. How many fighters could have gotten to their feet before the count of ten after catching Joe Frazier's full swing left hook flush on the jaw? Jimmy is one of the most overlooked heavyweight champions of the last four decades. This may be due in part because he boxed in the Ali - Frazier era. I've often wondered what the outcome may have been had Bob Foster challenged Ellis for the WBA title. Now that might be a dream match to run through a computer.

ZORA FOLLEY

Throughout the 1950's and 60's Zora Folley was among the best heavyweights in the world. Only a reluctant world champion and untimely losses kept him from getting a title shot in the prime of his career. It took Zora fourteen years before he received a crack at the championship. That would be against Muhammad Ali who at that time was at the peak of his powers.

Folley was born in Dallas, Texas on March 27, 1931. He would fight out of Arizona and turned professional in 1953. He was undefeated in his first nineteen bouts including two knockout victories over Howard King. In June of 1955 Folley suffered his first setback being halted by rugged Johnny Summerlin. Later that year Zora was stopped by Young Jack Johnson for the California heavyweight title. Folley would bounce back to win eighteen straight before he fought a draw with clever Eddie Machen in 1958. Among Zora's victims were Roger Rischer, Nino Valdes, Duke Sabadong and Wayne Bethea twice. Folley was now high in the heavyweight rankings.

Folley would continue in 1958 by taking out Pete Rademacher in four. Then Folley was surprisingly outpointed by England's Henry Cooper. Zora would return to England to defeat Joe Bygraves starting a ten fight win streak. During that streak he beat Alex Miteff, Willi Besmanoff, King again and Machen in a rematch. That led to a 1960 match with the feared Sonny Liston. It was a disaster for Folley. Liston was at his peak, and he manhandled Zora in three rounds. Then in 1961 Folley lost in seven to Alejandro Lavorante. Folley would again resurrect his career by winning nine in a row. Henry Cooper would fall in two rounds in a return bout. Zora also defeated Mike DeJohn, Robert Cleroux and Doug Jones. In a rematch with Jones in Madison Square Garden, Zora was knocked out in the seventh, another serious setback for Folley. In 1963 Zora would again outscore Cleroux. Then Folley lost a one sided decision to Ernie Terrell. Zora would then win four straight including a verdict over George Chuvalo. Next Folley fought a draw with Karl Mildenberger in Germany. Fighting his way back to the top of the ratings, Folley won seven in a row beating Oscar Bonevena, Bob Foster and Henry Clark.

Finally Zora would receive his long overdue title shot. On March 22, 1967, Folley challenged Muhammad Ali at Madison Square Garden. The aging Folley gave a good account of himself, but Ali was just too much for him. The bout and dream ended in round seven. Zora had ten fights after the loss to Ali. He went 5-3-2 losing to Brian London and Bonavena in a return. Folley's career ended when he was knocked down six times in the first round by undefeated Mac Foster.

Zora had 96 bouts in his formidable career. His final tally was 79-11-6. He won 44 by knockout, and he was halted 7 times. He fought four world champions and eight men who challenged for the crown. Folley died on July 7, 1972, from injuries following a poolside accident. He was only 41 years old.

MAC FOSTER

Long before Mark McGwire was launching tape measure home runs in Oakland and acquiring the nickname "Big Mac", West Coast sports fans used to cheer the feats of another "Big Mac". MacArthur Foster, a heavyweight boxer from Fresno, California, won his first 24 professional bouts all by knockout. Six came in the first round, four in the second round and seven in the third round. By the spring of 1970, he was the number one rated contender for Joe Frazier's crown.

Mac turned pro in November of 1966, and by the end of 1967, he had racked up nine kayos. Among his victims were veterans Floyd Joyner and Roy "Cookie" Wallace. He piled up seven more kayos in 1968, and in 1969, he made some serious noise in the heavyweight ratings. With Muhammad Ali banned from boxing, Joe Frazier and Jimmy Ellis shared the heavyweight crown. The division needed some new blood, and many felt Foster was the answer. Mac added six more knockouts in 1969 stopping Roger Rischer, Thad Spencer, Roger Russell, Cleveland Williams (twice) and Bob Felstein. Although Williams was well past his prime, he could still punch, and Mac took all he had to offer and came back to win both times.

After stopping Jack O'Halloran in one round on April 9th, 1970, for his 24th straight kayo victory, Mac decided to come east to New York. In his Madison Square Garden debut, he was to take on veteran contender Jerry Quarry. A victory over Quarry would no doubt ensure a big money fight with Frazier. On June 17th, as Jerry Quarry was to do several times during his exciting career, he upset the odds stopping a tentative Foster in six rounds. Quarry out boxed his less experienced foe until lowering the boom in the sixth. Mac showed none of his storied power. Quarry used the Foster victory as a springboard to match with the returning Muhammad Ali. Three months later, Mac returned to stop shopworn ex-contender Zora Folley in one round. Mac rolled off three more victories and then signed to meet Muhammad Ali. Ali had lost to Joe Frazier in the March 8, 1971, "Battle of the Century". Now Ali was taking on all new comers proclaiming himself to be the "People's Champion". Mac met Ali on April 1st, 1972, in Tokyo, Japan. Although Mac went the fifteen round distance, Ali won by a very comfortable margin. Mac looked slow and ponderous and did not show the power of a fighter with a record of 28-1, all 28 wins by knockout coming into this contest.

The loss to Ali was probably the highlight of Mac's career. He would score knockouts over journeymen Sam McGill and Charley Williams. Then he was out hustled over ten rounds by Bob Stallings. Mac closed out 1973 dropping a ten round duke in England to Joe Bugner. Foster had one fight in 1974 being outscored by slick Henry Clark. Mac took 1975 off and had his last bout in 1976 losing a ten rounder to Stan Ward.

Although overrated at the beginning of his career, Mac proved to be a competent fighter. He finished with a 30-6 record, all wins coming by knockout, and he was only stopped once. Mac's biggest claim to fame may have been in a late 1960's sparring session when he reportedly flattened Charles "Sonny" Liston!

JOSE LUIS GARCIA

There may have never been a more talent rich period in the heavyweight division then from 1968 to 1978. With Muhammad Ali (a.k.a. Cassius Clay) on the sidelines due to his draft case, other big men emerged. They would compete with each other on an almost equal basis for the next decade. Joe Frazier had risen to the top of the heap, but the level below him would remain as mainstays in the ratings for years to come.

Jimmy Ellis, Jerry Quarry, Oscar Bonevena, Floyd Patterson, George Chuvalo and Henry Cooper would eventually give way to Ron Lyle, Joe Bugner, Ken Norton, Earnie Shavers and Jimmy Young. All-time great champions like George Foreman and Larry Holmes also made their mark, and Ali re-emerged to reclaim his throne.

Lost among the giants of that time period was a fine heavyweight from Venezuela named Jose Luis Garcia. Although Jose never challenged for the world championship, he did meet three who did. He also met three world champions in a career that never seemed to reach its full potential.

Jose turned pro in his native country in 1968. He would go undefeated in his first nine bouts before losing a decision to future light heavyweight champion Vincente Rondon. Three fights later, Jose was halted by tough Allen Thomas in his first U.S. appearance. The lean Garcia was beginning to grow into a full-fledged heavyweight. On July 2, 1970, Garcia scored the biggest victory of his career. In Los Angeles as a heavy underdog, Jose met unbeaten and upcoming future champion Ken Norton. Garcia's superior hand speed and deceptive power sent Norton crashing in round eight.

The huge upset of Norton landed Garcia smack in the middle of the heavyweight picture. Four months later Garcia halted used up ex contender Thad Spencer. By now Garcia was gaining substantial weight. He was by today's standards a cruiserweight when he beat Norton. Now he was ballooning to well over 200 pounds. In 1971 he moved up in the ratings with wins over veterans Charlie Polite, James J. Woody, John Griffin and

Alberto Lovell. Jose opened 1973 with victories over Roby Harris, Florida Al Jones and Johnny Hudgins.

It all came crashing down on October 23, 1972, when ex World Boxing Association champion Ernie Terrell came to Caracas. Ernie had been written off after late 1960's losses to Thad Spencer and Manuel Ramos. Against Garcia though, he looked the part of a rejuvenated former champion as he pounded Garcia into submission in the sixth round. In Jose's comeback bout seven months later, Joe Alexander destroyed him in one round. What came next was a crushing kayo loss to Ron Lyle. Jose put together four wins but then lost a decision to Jimmy Young. In his next bout, Joe Bugner stopped him in two. Finally on August 14, 1975, Jose got a rematch with Ken Norton. At this time Norton was the top heavyweight contender. They met in St. Paul, Minnesota. This time Kenny took all Garcia could throw at him and eventually wore Jose down and stopped him in the fifth round of a tough fight. Even in defeat, Garcia proved he was still world class.

GEORGE "SCRAP IRON" JOHNSON

He only won 22 of 54 professional contests in a career that spanned seventeen years. He still became one of the most recognizable heavyweight "journeymen" of his era, although his record is dotted with losses. It looks like a who's who of the heavyweight division during the 1960's and 70's. He battled three world champions and seven men who fought for the heavyweight title along with one who fought the great Bob Foster for the light heavyweight title. He also faced ten others who, at one point or another, were considered legitimate contenders.

George "Scrap Iron" Johnson was only 5' 9" tall, so he was usually at a disadvantage against the big heavyweights. Still he took on all comers. He began his career in 1958 and had his last fight in 1975 when he was stopped in five rounds by the then up and coming Duane Bobick.

In only his sixth pro fight, he met future contender Tod Herring and was stopped in six. In 1964 he suffered losses to Andy Kendall and Thad Spencer. In 1965 he lost to Amos "Big Train" Lincoln, Henry Clark and Elmer Rush. He also fought to a draw with Mexican heavyweight Manuel Ramos.

In 1966 he was stopped in two by a young Jerry Quarry. He also went the distance in a losing effort against the talented Eddie Machen. In 1967 he took the streaking Joe Frazier the full ten rounds. Johnson then went on a six bout win streak.

In 1969 Johnson met the returning Sonny Liston and was stopped in seven. He then went ten rounds in a rematch with Quarry. Future champion George Foreman halted him, but he then went the full route with Joe Bugner. In 1971 he went out in two rounds against Jurgen Blin. In 1972 big, bad Ron Lyle took his measure in three.

George put four wins together, but then he lost consecutive decisions to Boone Kirkman, Johnny Boudreaux, Quarry and Leroy Jones. In 1975 he drew with the rugged Scott LeDoux, but then the loss to Bobick came and the end of his career.

Scrap Iron was a tough and rugged guy. He was the kind of fighter you had to beat if you hoped to raise your game to the serious contender level.

BILLY JOINER

In the early 1960's Cincinnati produced what looked to be a blue chip heavyweight prospect. Billy Joiner turned professional in 1962 after a stellar amateur career. He won 86 of 92 fights in the amateur ranks winning the National AAU and Golden Gloves light heavyweight titles in 1962. He twice crossed gloves with none other than Cassius Clay.

After turning professional, Billy won his first seven fights. Marion Conner, Amos Johnson and Lou Bailey were among the men he defeated. In 1964 he lost his first fight, a ten round decision to Amos Johnson for the Ohio State heavyweight title. Joiner was then stopped by Hubert Hilton and outscored by Jimmy "The King" Fletcher. Billy then fought three straight draws against Piero Tomasoni, Dante Cane and Chuck Leslie.

In 1968 Joiner would go to Los Angeles to face the feared former heavyweight champion Sonny Liston. Sonny had embarked on a comeback and was slowly working his way back into the ratings. Billy was halted in round seven. Ten months later Joiner would meet Sonny again, this time in St. Louis. The game and crafty Joiner extended Sonny the full ten rounds in losing a decision.

In his next bout Billy would score a major upset outpointing Canadian Robert Cleroux eliminating Cleroux from a proposed title match with World Boxing Association heavyweight champion Jimmy Ellis. The tide turned quickly though as Joiner would lose his next seven fights. It was against some stiff competition though, like Zora Folley, Alvin "Blue" Lewis, Juergen Blin, Mac Foster, Bernd August, Larry Holmes and Oscar Bonavena. Billy did gain some measure of revenge halting Fletcher in a rematch. A one round KO loss to Alfredo Evangalista followed that. Joiner didn't fight again for three and a half years, but closed his career with a victory outscoring Young Louis in Detroit.

Joiner finished his career with a 12-13-3 record. It is a very deceiving record. Along the way he met two world champions and three others that challenged for the crown. Add in legitimate contenders like Mac Foster and "Blue" Lewis and you can see Billy boxed with some of the best.

AL JONES

Lost in the shuffle among all the <u>heavyweight</u> greats of the 1960's and 1970's were names like Alvin "Blue" Lewis, Larry Middleton, Henry Clark and "Florida" Al Jones. Please don't confuse "Florida" Al with journeyman "Memphis" Al Jones. Those two settled their superiority issue in August of 1967 with "Florida" Al winning in three rounds.

After losing his pro debut with Duke Johnson in June of 1964, "Florida" reeled off 24 straight victories. He beat the "Duke" in a rematch. He also scored two victories over Chip Johnson and two kayos over Levi Forte. He decisioned Jefferson Davis and Bob Stallings and halted Sonny Moore, Archie Ray and stopped James J. Beattie in one round. Trained by Angelo Dundee, Jones sparred many rounds with Muhammad Ali and Jimmy Ellis.

The streak was ended when Al drew with veteran contender Zora Folley in May of 1968. He then won six more bouts including knockouts of Cleveland Williams and Jack O'Halloran plus a point win over Henry Clark.

By now Al was firmly entrenched in the lower tier of the Top Ten with only one loss and one draw on his record. On January 27, 1970, Luis Pires held Al to a draw. It was a fight in which Jones broke his hand for the first of four occasions. He didn't step into the ring again until October 25, 1971, when he outscored Roy "Cookie" Wallace suffering hand break number two along the way. Six months later he dropped a ten round verdict in Venezuela to Jose Luis Garcia while suffering his third break. It would be over three years before he fought again, and that was a one round kayo victory.

From January of 1970 until February of 1976 when Al out fought the capable Jody Ballard, Jones had fought only five times. The inactivity and another broken hand finally caught up to him when the erratic Tom Prater stopped him in six rounds. Jones, once a bright prospect, retired with a very formidable 33-3-3 record.

DOUG JONES

Doug Jones was a fighter who was good enough to challenge for world title recognition in two different weight classes. He also holds knockout victories over former world champions Bob Foster and Carl "Bobo" Olson. He was surely a major player during the 1960's.

In all, he met six world title holders. He also crossed gloves with top contenders like Eddie Machen, Pete Rademacher, Zora Folley, Billy Daniels, George Chuvalo, Thad Spencer and Boone Kirkman.

Impressive? You bet! Here's more. He gave "The Greatest", Cassius Clay (Muhammad Ali) his toughest pre championship fight, and to this day, there are many who feel that the decision rendered that night was a travesty.

For some people, timing is everything. Take Lennox Lewis and <u>Roy Jones Jr.</u>, who were talented boxers that were fortunate to come along when their respective divisions were void of serious challengers. Then take Jerry Quarry, who was a talented fighter, who happened to box in the greatest heavyweight era. Somehow it just doesn't seem fair.

Doug Jones suffered the same fate as Quarry. Bad timing with a dash of bad luck equals Doug Jones. However, Jones was no joke. Doug turned professional in 1958 and won his first nineteen fights facing light heavyweights as well as heavyweights. He established himself as a viable contender in 1960 with two wins over Von Clay and a six round KO of Bobo Olsen. His 1961 wins over Rademacher and another over Von Clay led the unbeaten Jones into a match with the highly rated Machen. Doug lost the verdict but little stature.

In his next bout Doug met the classy Harold Johnson for the vacant world light heavyweight championship. The clever Johnson out boxed Doug in this 1962 contest, and Jones dropped his next bout on points to Zora Folley. Showing the tenacity that molded his career, Doug bounced back to score kayos over Bob Foster and Folley in a return match.

On March 13, 1963, Doug took on the unbeaten and highly touted Olympic gold medalist Cassius Clay in a sold out jammed packed <u>Madison Square Garden</u>. It was the night that the roof almost caved in on young Cassius. Maybe he underestimated Doug. Who knows? The fact is that Doug hurt Cassius early and often. It didn't take Clay long to realize that he was in the fight of his life! By the middle rounds, Cassius was able to get his jab working. Only then did he climb back into the fight. The officials thought Clay did enough to win. The fans did not. Clay was booed without mercy, and Jones, who was short ended, received the cheers of a winner.

This would be the highlight of Doug's respectable career. There were ups but also untimely downs like the night Doug was upset by the rugged Canadian Chuvalo. He resurged with five straight kayo wins over mediocre opposition and was awarded a shot at the World Boxing Association heavyweight title held by Ernie Terrell.

On June 28th, 1966, Doug failed on his date with destiny as the bigger, taller Terrell won a boring points verdict to retain his bogus title. Four months later Doug was beaten by up and coming prospect Thad Spencer. Then on February 21st, 1967, Doug became a stepping-stone on Joe Frazier's march toward the heavyweight crown. You could see the end was near, but Doug had one more surprise left. He traveled to Seattle and upset their unbeaten prospect Boone Kirkman via a badly cut eye. Boone wanted Doug again and got him. The faded Jones was no match in the return as Kirkman got sweet revenge, and Doug got a ticket to retirement.

Doug lost ten of forty-one fights. These are not Hall Of Fame numbers. It is doubtful that Doug will ever get in the Hall, but it is a shame that his name is rarely mentioned when the top big men of the 60's are brought up. As time goes on, his stand against young Cassius is almost forgotten. Doug deserves better than that.

LEROY JONES

Over the years a very good heavyweight contender from the late 1970's and early 80's has been all but forgotten. Big Leroy Jones lost only one fight in his professional career that was to the great Larry Holmes.

Leroy was a two-time New York Golden Gloves champion who turned professional in 1973. A naturally big man, Leroy weighed 228 for his pro debut. He would go on to weigh 240 or more for future battles.

Nevertheless, he was light on his feet and a very smooth boxer. Many compared his style to former contender Buster Mathis Sr. Jones would reel off seventeen straight wins including victories over Larry Frazier (twice), Rico Brooks, Big Jim Gilmore (twice) and Jody Ballard. In 1976 he fought a ten round draw with another highly touted prospect, Pedro Lovell.

Leroy bounced back to put together a seven fight win streak that would carry him to a shot at the world's championship. He defeated rugged Dino Denis and won the North American Boxing Federation heavyweight title with a twelve round decision over future world titleholder Mike Weaver.

On March 31, 1980, Jones met Larry Holmes at Caesars Palace in Las Vegas for the <u>World Boxing Council</u>'s version of the heavyweight title. Larry dominated the action against the 254-pound Jones. The fight was stopped at 2:56 of round eight with Holmes retaining his title. Leroy was well behind on all three cards at the time of the stoppage. Jones also suffered a detached retina that would force him to retire for two years. Leroy came back in 1982 weighing in at 275 pounds. He halted Jeff Shelburg in two rounds, and that was Leroy's last fight.

Jones ended up with a very formidable record of 25-1-1. He won thirteen contests via the kayo route. He was among the top ten heavyweights in the world for over a three-year period.

BOONE KIRKMAN

Way back in the 1960's boxing fans and the media still searched for a heavyweight "White Hope". There was Jerry Quarry and George Chuvalo along with the likes of Tony Doyle, etc...In 1966 a fighter emerged from the upper northwest region of the United States. He was strong, aggressive and packed a wallop. He was quickly added to the White Hope bandwagon. His name was Daniel Victor Kirkman, but to his adoring fans he was "Boone".

Kirkman was born January 1, 1945, and resided in Renton, Washington. In 1966 he turned professional after winning the National

A.A.U. heavyweight title in 1965. The wily old manager Jack Hurley viewed Kirkman as a diamond in the rough and took him under his wing. Boone would win six fights in his maiden year including two decisions over Archie Ray.

Kirkman started 1967 by winning five straight including a three round stoppage over faded contender Eddie Machen. The streak ended when Kirkman suffered his first loss on cuts to veteran contender Doug Jones. Boone turned the tables in their rematch halting Jones in round six. In 1968 Kirkman beat journeymen Aaron Eastling and Bill McMurray. He would not fight in 1969 due to an injury. He returned in 1970 to win four in a row including a two round knockout over Amos "Big Train" Lincoln.

On November 18, 1970, Kirkman made his Madison Square Garden debut. His opponent would be the undefeated 1968 Olympic Gold Medal winner George Foreman. The fans settled in expecting a slugfest. What they got was a massacre. Foreman pushed down, shoved and manhandled poor Boone. The one sided affair ended in round two. Kirkman's stock dropped dramatically.

To Kirkman's credit he would come back to win ten in a row into 1974. He defeated the giant Jack O'Halloran and George "Scrapiron" Johnson. He pulled himself off the canvas to win a split decision over former champion Jimmy Ellis. Boone was now back in the ratings. A stop over tune up in Dallas proved to be an ambush as Kirkman was creamed in the third round by Memphis Al Jones, a fighter with a 6-21-2 record. Most chalked it up to a lucky punch KO, and Boone moved on to meet the highly rated Ken Norton. Kirkman's style was made for Ken as he broke Boone down and halted him in seven. Next Kirkman took on the dangerous Ron Lyle. The hard hitting Lyle busted Boone up and stopped him in eight.

On April 26, 1975, Kirkman agreed to be one of five boxers to face now former heavyweight champion George Foreman. The circus like festivities saw an out of shape Foreman getting by his first four foes. His last opponent would be Kirkman. Foreman hurt Boone and floored him in the first, but could not finish him. Boone lasted the three round distance and even landed a few good shots. Kirkman showed guts and resolve by refusing to let Foreman stop him again. Later in 1975 Kirkman would fall completely out of the rankings dropping a ten round verdict to the clever Randy Neumann.

In 1977 Kirkman returned to defeat Joe "King" Roman, Ron Stander and Pedro Agosto. In 1978 Boone would fight his last battle beating Charles Atlas. Kirkman would retire with a formidable 36-6 record. He had 25 KO's and he was stopped five times. I believe he was still among the Top Twenty heavyweights in the world when he decided to hang them up. He fought three world champions and five boxers who challenged for a title.

SCOTT LEDOUX

Scott LeDoux of Minnesota was a heavyweight contender in the 1970's and 80's. He was a game and rugged customer who crossed gloves with some of the best the heavyweight division had to offer during his era.

In his fifty-bout career, Scott met eight heavyweight champions.....
EIGHT! They were George Foreman, Leon Spinks, Ken Norton, Mike Weaver, Gerrie Coetzee, Frank Bruno, Larry Holmes and Greg Page. On July 7, 1980, Scott met Larry Holmes for the WBC title. He was stopped in seven rounds. In addition to meeting eight champs, he also fought three men who challenged for crown. They were Ron Lyle, Terry Daniels and Ron Stander. He also met other worthy contenders like Duane and Rodney Bobick, Marty Monroe, Dino Dennis, Larry Middleton and Johnny Boudreaux. Scott's bout with Boudreaux stands out. It was part of the United States Boxing Tourney. LeDoux lost a very debatable decision. A little scuffle ensued, and somewhere in melee, Howard Cosell's toupee was dislodged. Fond memories... My favorite LeDoux fight was his battle with Ken Norton. Well behind on points, the gutsy LeDoux mounted a rally to close the gap. He had Norton out on his feet at the final bell. The

bout ended in a draw. After his career ended, Scott did some fine work as a TV commentator. He later served as the Minnesota boxing commissioner.

ALVIN "BLUE" LEWIS

The late 60's and early 70's spawned an array of fistic talent in the heavyweight division, from the great champions Patterson, Liston, Ali, Frazier and Foreman along with Ellis and Terrell to the parade of bonafide contenders. Almost always among the top contenders of the day were the names of Chuvalo, Quarry, Bonevena, Norton, Lyle, Shavers, Bugner, Leotis Martin and Henry Clark. Throw in a Mac Foster, Boone Kirkman and Chuck Wepner and you get an idea of the talented mix. Among the elite during this time was a fine fighter out of Michigan named Al "Blue" Lewis. It is conceivable that if "Blue" would have boxed in a different era, he may have become a champion.

Lewis turned pro in 1966 and quickly racked up eight straight victories that year. He continued to roll in 1967 winning six more. Among his victims were veterans Aaron Eastling, Willie McMillan and Dick Wipperman. Lewis would take his win streak to twenty. Three times he defeated rugged Bob Stallings. He also scored a huge victory stopping highly regarded Eduardo Corletti in two rounds. People began to take Lewis seriously as a legitimate contender.

The bubble burst on November 26, 1968, when Lewis soared to an early lead over veteran Leotis Martin but faded down the stretch, the bout being stopped in the ninth round. Three months later, Al again failed to beat the clever Martin dropping a ten round decision.

Lewis spent the rest of 1969 and 1970 trying to re-establish himself. He won six straight including a kayo win over Cleveland Williams. On October 4, 1971, "Blue" traveled to Argentina to meet Oscar Bonevena. He returned with a seventh round disqualification loss. Many felt that Al was getting the better of Oscar at the time of the stoppage. His performance against Bonevena was good enough to get Al a shot at Muhammad Ali.

The former champion was fighting all the contenders trying to eliminate them to force a rematch with titleholder Joe Frazier. The Ali-Lewis contest took place on July 19, 1972, in Dublin, Ireland. Muhammad struggled with Lewis before scoring a knockdown in the middle rounds. Lewis rallied back, but Ali finally ended matters in the eleventh round.

Lewis came back in 1973 beating Charlie Reno but then lost a surprising verdict to Big Jack O'Halloran. Lewis then scored three straight kayo victories over mediocre opponents. He then decided to hang up the gloves finishing with a 30-6 record. Today "Blue" is a respected trainer in Detroit.

BRIAN LONDON

The British produced some quality heavyweights in the 1950's and into the 1960's. Of course the very popular Henry Cooper comes to mind. There was Joe Erskine and Billy "Golden Boy" Walker. One of the best was rugged Brian London who twice challenged for world honors some of the best heavyweights in the world in his fine career.

Brian was born in 1934 and turned professional in 1955. He won his first twelve bouts, eleven by knockout, before being stopped in one round by Henry Cooper in 1956. Brian bounced back to win eight of his next nine before dropping a decision to the clever Willie Pastrano in 1958. Three months later, London would halt Joe Erskine in eight rounds to win the British and Commonwealth heavyweight titles. He would then stop Pastrano on cuts in a rematch.

Brian was now a serious contender for a world title shot. In 1959 he lost his titles by decision to Henry Cooper. Nevertheless he was awarded a shot at Floyd Patterson's heavyweight title. After a valiant effort, Floyd stopped London in eleven rounds. Brian would then be stopped in seven by the dangerous Nino Valdes.

In 1960 London would halt former Olympic gold medalist Pete Rademacher. Later in the year, Dick Richardson would stop Brian in his attempt to win the European title. In 1961 the highly rated Eddie Machen kayoed London in five. In 1962 he dropped a decision to Santo Amonti.

In 1963 Brian would lose a twelve round decision to former world champion Ingemar Johansson. It would be Ingo's last fight. In 1964 he again lost a fifteen rounder to Henry Cooper with the European, British and Commonwealth titles on the line. He then lost to up and coming Johnny Prescott but amazingly rebounded to defeat Chip Johnson, Billy Walker and Roger Rischer.

In 1966 he dropped a decision to a very talented Thad Spencer. Later in the year, Brian received his second shot at immortality when he met Muhammad Ali for the world's title. In one of young Ali's best performances, he battered the badly overmatched London in three rounds. Brian would continue on. He lost a tough decision to the highly touted Jerry Quarry. He then defeated highly regarded Zora Folley. In 1968 he suffered damaging kayo losses to Roberto Davila and Jack Bodell. Although he drew with Henry Clark in 1969, he later lost to Jimmy "The King" Fletcher and was taken out in two in a return bout with Quarry.

In 1970 Brian was taken out in five by rising star Joe Bugner and that ended his career. London engaged in 58 professional contests. He won 37 of them, 26 by knockout. He fought four world champions, Ali, Patterson, Johansson and Pastrano. He met six boxers that fought for world title honors in Henry Cooper, Pete Rademacher, Eddie Machen, Jerry Quarry, Zora Folley and Joe Bugner. He also met other top notch guys like Nino Valdes, Thad Spencer and Henry Clark, just to name a few. Brian London had a very respectable career, and he did England proud.

RON LYLE

Big, strong Ron Lyle was a heavyweight who fought during the talent rich 1970's. He was a main stream contender for nearly a decade. He fought "The Greatest", Muhammad Ali, for the title and more then held his own until being stopped in round eleven. He had "Big" George Foreman on the

31

canvas twice before succumbing to George's <u>power</u> in probably one of the best heavyweight battles of all time. His all action shoot out with Earnie Shavers would be a strong runner up to his bout with Foreman.

Ron started his career late after serving 7 ½ years in prison. It did not take him long to establish himself. Wins over Manuel Ramos, Jack O'Halloran, Vincente Rondon, Buster Mathis, Luis Pires and Larry Middleton moved him up quickly in the ratings. Granted that Ramos was a washed up former contender and O'Halloran was a fringe contender, Rondon was a former light heavyweight title claimant until "Bad" Bobby Foster drilled that dream out of his head. Middleton was a game and clever boxer who just happened to lack a punch. Pires was a decent heavyweight from South America. Nevertheless this impressive win streak sent him into a bout with Jerry Quarry. The hard luck, Quarry was on the downside of his career and had recently suffered his second loss to Muhammad Ali. On this night though, Jerry's experience and Lyle's lack of it was clearly evident. Quarry took Ron to counter punching school and handed Lyle his first loss. Even in defeat Ron showed his gameness. Overmatched at this stage of his career, he hung tough and learned his lessons well.

To Ron's credit, he quickly went back to the business of re-establishing himself with a win and a draw against clever Gregorio Peralta and pulverizing knockouts over the very dangerous Jose Luis Garcia, Jurgen Blin and hard hitting Boone Kirkman. Then came a decision win over Larry Middleton in a rematch. Twelve round verdicts over the clever former champion Jimmy Ellis and rugged Oscar Bonevena put Lyle back in the title picture. His only loss during this time was a decision setback against slick boxing Jimmy Young. Ron finally challenged Muhammad Ali for the world's championship that Ali had regained the year before when he "Rope-a-Doped" the Mummy, George Foreman.

Ali tried to use that same tactic against Lyle, but Ron would have none of it. Forcing Ali to box at ring center, Lyle was able to trade evenly with Ali in a very slow paced bout. For a big and strong guy, Ron was a decent boxer. He was not a good enough boxer though to match wits with Ali,

Young or even Quarry. In hindsight Ron should have fought a different fight. He should been more aggressive and taken chances. In round eleven Ali stunned Lyle and trapped him in a corner. Ali's follow up barrage had Ron out on his feet when the referee intervened. Ron would never receive another shot at the title, very unfair based on his credentials. Lyle's bout with Shavers was a slugfest. Ron got up off the canvas to score a brutal knockout. The brawl with Foreman was a classic for the ages. It pitted two of the biggest, strongest men ever to lace on a boxing glove. They traded bombs with each other with no regard for defense. It was a savage war of attrition in which both men tasted the canvas. Lyle finally fell for good in round five.

The loss to Foreman and another decision loss to the clever Jimmy Young forced Ron to rally toward another title shot. Hard fought decision wins over Joe Bugner, Stan Ward and Scott LeDoux again put Ron on contention. A surprising second round kayo loss to unheralded Lynn Ball dropped Ron from consideration. In his last significant bout, Gerry Cooney halted Ron in one round. Ron made a brief comeback years later, but it was in the 70's that Lyle made his mark.

EDDIE MACHEN

He was one of the best heavyweights of his era and possibly one of the best heavyweights to have never claimed the title. He fought the best of the late 1950's and 60's with a high degree of success.

Eddie Machen was born on July 15, 1932, in Redding, California, and he entered the punch for pay ranks in 1955. Eddie won all eleven of his bouts during his maiden year including a knockout over highly regarded Howard King.

In 1956 Eddie added eight more victories and established himself as a force to be reckoned with in the heavyweight division. He twice defeated Julio Mederos and also won two bouts against the dangerous Nino Valdes. Eddie closed 1956 with a points victory over tough Johnny Summerlin.

Machen opened 1957 with a pair of wins over the clever former light heavyweight champion Joey Maxim of Cleveland. He also defeated Bob Baker and closed the year with a kayo over Tommy "Hurricane" Jackson. Eddie was now a leading contender for Floyd Patterson's heavyweight title.

It was in 1958 that the fortunes of Eddie Machen's career began to take a turn. He opened the year by battling to a draw with the slick Zora Folley. Then came the bout that shocked the boxing world. Eddie traveled to Sweden to meet Ingemar Johansson. The fight would last only 2:16, but it would thrust Ingo into a title fight against Patterson and leave Eddie on a long waiting list. Ingo would upset Floyd to win the crown, and then Patterson would roar back to regain it. That would set up a rubber match that Floyd would win. From the time Eddie lost to Ingo and the conclusion of the Patterson-Johansson trilogy, two and a half years had passed.

After the loss to Ingo, Eddie won seven straight, and then was matched again with Zora Folley. This time Zora got the verdict. Machen rebounded with three more wins including Alex Miteff and Alonzo Johnson among his victims.

On September 7, 1960, Eddie stepped into the ring to face the feared Sonny Liston. To many, Liston was the "Uncrowned Heavyweight Champion", and a bout with Patterson was being called for by the fans and press alike. Only Eddie stood in Sonny's way. The bout took place in Seattle, and Eddie gave the brutish Liston all he could handle. In the end Sonny took a unanimous decision despite losing three points for low blows. Nevertheless, Eddie's game showing won him the admiration of boxing fans. Despite the win over the highly ranked Machen, Sonny would have to wait two more years to get Patterson into the ring with him.

Eddie would come back to win three in a row, but then he was upset over ten rounds by the cagey Harold Johnson. Machen would regroup and put together a streak of ten wins and one draw. The draw was with the murderous punching Cleveland Williams. Among the boxers Eddie beat during this streak, were Mike DeJohn, Brian London, Doug Jones and

Bert Whitehurst. This finally led Eddie to the ghost that had long eluded him, Floyd Patterson.

By now it was 1964, and Eddie returned to Sweden, the place of his disastrous loss to Johansson to face Floyd. This was one of Patterson's best career performances as he won a hard fought decision over Machen. Still Eddie had done well enough to qualify for a title fight.

On March 5, 1965, Eddie met tall, lanky Ernie Terrell for the "vacant" World Boxing Association title. Cassius Clay, a.k.a., Muhammad Ali, had been stripped of his title by the WBA. The Terrell-Machen battle was not a good pairing of styles, and, after a rather boring fifteen rounds, Terrell was awarded the championship. Eddie would close 1965 by drawing with Elmer Rush.

Machen would open 1966 with back to back decision losses to Karl Mildenberger and Manuel Ramos. He would then outfight the tough Joey Orbillo. Next Eddie would show flashes of his former greatness and pull off a major upset with a points win over top prospect Jerry Quarry.

Two fights after the upset of Quarry, Eddie would meet another streaking prospect 1964 Olympic champion Joe Frazier. This time Lady Luck looked the other way for Eddie, and he was halted by "Smokin' Joe" in the tenth round.

Machen was now relegated to the role of a trail horse. In 1967 he dropped a decision to up and coming Henry Clark. In his last professional fight, Eddie was stopped in three by hard hitting Boone Kirkman.

In all Eddie had 64 pro fights. He won 50 of them. He took out 29 opponents. He fought champions Liston, Patterson, Johansson, Terrell, Frazier, Maxim and Harold Johnson. He also did battle with top contenders like Zora Folley, Cleveland Williams, Alex Mitiff, Mike DeJohn, Willie Besmanoff, Doug Jones, Tommy Jackson, Nino Valdes, Karl Mildenberger, Jerry Quarry, Bob Baker, Bert Whitehurst, Howard King, Henry Clark, Julio Mederos, Joey Orbillo, Brian London, Wayne Bethea and Boone Kirkman. That is very impressive!

Eddie Machen was only forty years old when he left this world. It was only five years after his last fight, but he left a legacy that will live forever.

LEOTIS MARTIN

The great city of Philadelphia has produced several fine champions and contenders over the years. One boxer from Philly aspired to be the heavyweight champion of the world. He fell short of his goal as an eye injury ended his career. He sure went out with a bang though. His name was Leotis Martin, and he was a ranked contender throughout most of the late 1960's.

Leotis was born March 10, 1939. He had a stellar amateur career and turned professional in 1962. Martin won his first nine bouts, but in 1963, he was halted by Floyd McCoy. Leotis bounced right back to win fifteen straight contests that took him into 1967. Martin defeated Dave Bailey, Don Warner, Sonny Banks, Von Clay, Amos Johnson, Roberto Davila and Billy Daniels. The bout with Banks on May 10, 1965, in Philadelphia ended tragically as Sonny died due to injuries sustained in the fight. Banks had been the first boxer in the pro ranks to put Cassius Clay on the seat of his pants.

In 1967 Muhammad Ali was stripped of the heavyweight title for refusing to go into the United States Army. The World Boxing Association then held an eight man elimination tournament to find Ali's successor. Martin was one of the eight contestants. On August 5, 1967, at the Houston Astrodome, Martin met former amateur foe Jimmy Ellis. In the very first round Ellis rocked Martin with a booming right hand. Leotis made it through the round, but on this day, Ellis just seemed a little bit sharper than Leotis. The fight was stopped in the ninth round as Martin was badly cut inside his mouth. Ellis would go on to decision Oscar Bonavena and Jerry Quarry to win the tournament.

In his very next bout, Martin was upset by Roger Russell. Leotis rebounded to take out Karl Mildenberger in seven. Martin then lost a decision to a talented upstart named Henry Clark. Martin got back on the winning track stopping Thad Spencer in London, England. Reports say this bout was a real donnybrook. Spencer had also participated in the Eight Man Tourney. Thad upset former World Boxing Association titleholder Ernie Terrell in his first tournament bout. In his next one Spencer was halted in the final round by Jerry Quarry. The bout in London between Martin and Spencer was a true crossroads contest for both men.

Martin would next travel to Argentina where he dropped a decision to rugged Oscar Bonavena. Leotis would then score two victories over the highly regarded prospect Alvin "Blue" Lewis. Martin then knocked out Wendell Newton and beat Roger Russell in a rematch. At this time the comeback of former world champion Sonny Liston was kicking into high gear. Sonny had been impressive taking apart Henry Clark. He was back in the rankings and looking for a title shot. On December 6, 1969, Leotis and Sonny would meet in Las Vegas. At stake would be the newly created North American Boxing Federation heavyweight title. The bout was scheduled for twelve rounds. It was a slow paced fight that Sonny controlled through the first five rounds. He even decked Leotis in the fourth round. By the sixth round though, there was a subtle change as Leotis began to come on. He was actually starting to out jab Liston. By the eighth round Sonny still had the lead, but he was beginning to tire. A cut under his nose was bleeding freely, and the blood flowed into his mouth impairing his breathing. Then in the ninth, lightning struck. Sonny was using his jab trying to keep Martin off of him. Leotis threw a perfectly timed right over the jab that froze Sonny when it landed. A follow up left hook sent Liston face first to the canvas. Sonny was out cold. Leotis Martin had just knocked out Charles "Sonny" Liston.

Finally Leotis Martin appeared to be on the threshold of a world title fight. It seems like one thing Leotis didn't have was luck. During the Liston bout, Martin suffered a detached retina. Today surgery could have corrected that problem. In 1969 there was not much that could be done. Leotis had to retire. In his career he was 31-5 with 19 knockouts. Martin passed away on November 20, 1995. Leotis will always be remembered as the man who bombed out Sonny!

BUSTER MATHIS

At one time, Buster Mathis, Sr. of Grand Rapids, Michigan was the best amateur heavyweight in the world. This was in 1964, after he had twice defeated another promising amateur named Joe Frazier. He was on his way to the 1964 Olympics Games in Tokyo, but an injury sidelined him. Frazier took his place as an alternate. Joe won the Gold Medal, and the rest is history.

Where does Buster Mathis stand in the annals of heavyweight history? Did he ever get the respect that he may have deserved? He was a good enough prospect to have Cus D'Amato guide his professional career. He was a very big man for his era and was surprisingly fast and agile for a man his size.

At the beginning of his pro career, the 300 pound Mathis had shed weight and subdued opponents. In his fourth fight he would outpoint a rugged customer named Bob Stallings. In his sixth fight he would halt Chuck Wepner.

Buster was built up like most prospects at that time were. His record is spotted with journeymen like Charlie Polite, Mike Bruce, Everett Copeland, Sonny Moore...After 23 straight victories he was matched with old foe Joe Frazier for the New York State recognition of the heavyweight title that had been taken from Muhammad Ali.

This time Joe would have more rounds to work over and wear down Big Buster. Finally in the eleventh round Buster went down, and Joe had a piece of the heavyweight pie.

After the loss to Frazier, Mathis put together a nice five bout win streak. He beat Mel Turnbow, James J. Beattie, Amos "Big Train" Lincoln, Dick

Wipperman and James J. Woody. That was pretty respectable opposition at that time. This led to another shot at the big time, a match with the brawling Canadian contender George Chuvalo.

The bout with Chuvalo would be the highlight of Buster's fine career. If anyone ever doubts that Buster was a world class heavyweight, get a hold of the film of this fight. Mathis was the master of Chuvalo throughout the twelve round contest.

The win over Chuvalo had put Buster right back in the thick of the heavyweight picture. By this time the once 300 pound Mathis was tipping the scales around 235. Six weeks after the Chuvalo triumph, Buster would take on the erratic but always entertaining Jerry Quarry. On the night they fought Quarry was nothing short of brilliant. It was a boxing clinic, and Buster was soundly defeated. At this point Buster took some time off after a high profile loss.

It would be well over two years before Buster would re-enter the ring, and his opponent would be none other than the come backing Muhammad Ali. Buster had ballooned to over 250 pounds, and although game to the core, he was totally outclassed by Ali and lost a twelve round decision. This would finish Buster as a serious contender. Buster would defeat the undefeated Claude McBride, but in his next bout he was savaged by another unbeaten prospect named Ron Lyle. That would be the end of Buster's career. Big Buster only lost four of thirty four fights. He lost to Frazier, Quarry, Ali and Lyle. Does that make him all bad? The Buster Mathis that defeated George Chuvalo was one of the best heavyweights of the late 1960's.

DAN McALINDEN

In the early 1970's Dan McAlinden was a streaking young heavyweight. He appeared to have the makings of a world champion. He was strong, aggressive and packed a solid punch. He and Joe Bugner were both making noise in the heavyweight division. A battle between the two seemed inevitable.

McAlinden turned pro in 1969, and in his second pro fight he halted future British champion Richard Dunn. This is the same Dunn who would one day meet Muhammad Ali for the world title.

Danny would win his first eleven fights by knockout before suffering his first defeat. He dropped an eight round verdict to the underrated American Jack "The Giant" O' Halloran. Two fights later he drew with Ray "Brother of Floyd" Patterson. He also drew with Tommy Hicks a fighter he had previously beaten.

On March 8, 1971, on the under card of the classic Ali – Frazier I, Danny won a six round decision over Ali's brother Rahman Ali. That was the start of a six fight win streak for Danny. That streak ended when the talented Larry Middleton stopped Danny in eight. Three months later Danny would crush the soft chinned Jack Bodell in two rounds to win the British and Commonwealth heavyweight titles.

In 1973 Danny suffered a serious setback when hard punching Morris Jackson stopped him in three rounds. Up to that point Danny was being strongly considered as an opponent for new champion George Foreman's first title defense. After the loss to Jackson, Danny's career began to unravel. In 1974 Pat Duncan outscored him. In 1975 he lost his British and Commonwealth titles to the clever Bunny Johnson in nine rounds.

Richard Dunn defeated Bunny Johnson to win the titles, and in November of 1975 Danny met Dunn in an attempt to regain them. This time Richard Dunn was a different fighter then the one Danny had taken out in 1969. Dunn tasted sweet revenge as he floored Danny three times in the second round to retain his titles.

In 1976 unheralded Tony Moore stopped Danny in four rounds. In 1977 Neal Malpass halted him. In 1978 Tommy Kiely took him out in six rounds. In 1979 he lost a verdict to George Scott, and in 1980 he lost again to Tony Moore by decision.

Danny had his last fight in 1981 losing to Denton Ruddock in the fifth round. In all, Danny had 45 fights and posted a 31-12-2 record. He did win 28 by knockout. At one time a bout between Joe Bugner and Danny would have been the talk of the British Isles. Too bad it never came off.

JEFF MERRITT

He began his career in 1964, but it was not until 1973 that he crashed into the heavyweight ratings. In between were periods of inactivity and a multitude of meaningless bouts. He was a murderous punching prospect that no worthy opponent wanted to chance his career against. By the time he got his "shot" at the big time, he was 21-1 with 16 kayos. He scored seven first round kayos and eight second round stoppages. Yet up to this point, his claim to fame was being a <u>Muhammad Ali</u> sparring partner. It is a shame that today very few remember Jeff "Candy Slim" Merritt. True, his tenure as a mainstream contender was less than a year, but oh what a reputation he had. Many at that time considered him the hardest puncher in the heavyweight division bar none.

Although Jeff had one bout in 1964, his career really began in 1968. In 1969 Jeff established himself as a legitimate prospect with decision wins over Roy Williams, Roger Russell and Henry Clark. Finally on September 10th, 1973, Jeff stepped into the ring to face former World Boxing Association heavyweight champion Ernie Terrell. "Big" Ernie had held the W.B.A. title from 1965 to 1967 before losing a unification fight with Ali. He then lost to Thad Spencer in the W.B.A. eight-man elimination tourney and followed that with a loss to Mexican contender Manuel Ramos. An upset kayo victory over Jose Luis Garcia put Terrell back in the ratings. Despite a very controversial loss to Chuck Wepner, Ernie was still ranked when he faced Merritt. Less than one round later, Ernie was a retired ex-champion as Jeff destroyed him. Merritt followed this with a three round butchering of rugged Ron Stander.

Jeff kept his name in the headlines serving as Earnie Shavers sparring partner while Earnie prepared for his bout with Jerry Quarry. Archie Moore was training Shavers, and he allowed Merritt to spar with Earnie. A couple of vicious hooks caused the Quarry bout to be postponed as Earnie's jaw was broken. Don King, Earnie's manager, was livid. Archie was dismissed, and Quarry's trainer Gil Clancey said something to the effect that Merritt was the kind of guy you fought for money not in the gym.

All was going well until March 4th, 1974. Jeff faced old foe Henry Clark. This time Clark abandoned his usual cautious style and took Jeff by surprise. Jeff was now the victim of a one round kayo loss. The defeat put Jeff's career into a tail spin. It was almost 2 1/2 years before he would fight again. His opponent would be tough fringe contender Stan Ward. For two rounds Jeff out boxed the ponderous Ward shutting one of his eyes. In round three the half blind Ward connected, and again Jeff's chin betrayed him. The bout was soon stopped, and Ward had handed Jeff his ticket to boxing oblivion.

LARRY MIDDLETON

What would you say about a fighter who met the likes of Ken Norton, Ron Lyle, Jimmy Ellis, Jerry Quarry, Oscar Bonevena and Joe Bugner? These were all boxers who either held or fought for the world's heavyweight championship. Yet this fighter never came close to a world title shot. You could call him "Hard Luck". I would call him Larry Middleton.

Larry began his career in 1965 and didn't exactly set the world on fire. He drew with Jimmy Haynes in his pro debut, and two fights later, was stopped by Jerry O'Neal. He won three fights in a row in 1966 but was inactive in 1967. He won two fights in 1968 to bring his total of bouts to eight over a four-year period. Larry began to pick up the pace in 1969 winning a decision over dangerous Roy "Tiger" Williams. He followed with three more victories. He then added four more wins in 1970. In 1971 Larry scored two quick knockouts and then traveled to England to meet highly regarded Joe Bugner. At this time, Middleton owned a 16-1-1 record and had won fifteen in a row. Still no one really gave him a chance against Bugner. In a huge upset, Larry won a convincing decision and gained a world rating.

In 1972, Larry solidified his ranking with wins over Tony Doyle, Dan McAlinden and Bob Stallings. Back in England, Larry was matched with highly rated Jerry Quarry. Although Jerry won the ten round verdict, Larry gave him all he could handle. In Middleton's next fight, he was crushed in three rounds by an up and coming Ron Lyle. Ten months later on October 31, 1973, Larry met Lyle again. He went the distance but dropped a ten round verdict. Larry closed the year by halting Jack O'Halloran.

Middleton was still ranked in 1974, and on March 4th, he drew with former World Boxing Association champion Jimmy Ellis. Two months later Larry dropped a twelve round duke to long time contender Oscar Bonevena. 1975 started Larry on his way from contender to trial horse. A five round knockout loss to Howard "Kayo" Smith did severe damage to his career. In 1976 Larry dropped decisions to Duane Bobick and Scott Ledoux. In what would be his last chance in the limelight, Larry met Ken Norton on July 10th. In a game effort, Norton halted Larry in the tenth round, thus ending Middleton's run as a formidable contender.

KARL MILDENBERGER

Outside of former heavyweight champion Max Schmeling, Karl Mildenberger is the most popular heavyweight Germany has ever produced. Karl was born on November 23, 1937, and began his foray into professional boxing in 1958. He won his first eleven bouts, but in 1959, he suffered his first setback to Helmut Ball. Karl then went on to win his next nineteen bouts. Among his victims were Jimmy Slade, Franco Cavicchi, Harold Carter, Young Jack Johnson, Wayne Bethea, Howard King and Pete Rademacher.

On February 24, 1962, Mildenberger challenged Dick Richardson for the European Boxing Union title. Richardson shocked Karl stopping him in the very first round. Karl would bounce back to go unbeaten in his next twenty two contests. He fought draws with Archie McBride, Zora Folley and Amos Johnson. Mildenberger would defeat Joe Bygraves, Von Clay, Bethea again and McBride in a rematch. He also defeated Joe Erskine and Billy Daniels. On October 17, 1964, Karl would knock out Santo Amonti in one round to capture the European crown. Mildenberber made three successful defenses against Piero Tomasoni, Gerhard Zech and Ivan Prebeg. Karl also won a decision over Eddie Machen.

Finally Karl received a shot at the world's heavyweight championship. On September 10, 1966, Mildenberger took a lofty 49-2-3 record into the ring to face Muhammad Ali. It turned out to be a tough fight for the champion. Early on it seemed like Ali was a bit confused by Karl's southpaw style. As the fight progressed though Ali's size, speed and superior skills took over. Muhammad finally halted his stubborn challenger in round twelve. Karl has the distinction of being the first southpaw to fight for the heavyweight title.

Mildenberger returned to action defending his European title twice against Tomasoni and Billy Walker. He also stopped Amos "Big Train" Lincoln. Ali had been stripped of the heavyweight championship for refusing induction in to the United States Army. The World Boxing Association held a tournament to determine a new title holder. Eight boxers were chosen, and Mildenberger was one of them. His first opponent would be strong but crude Oscar Bonavena of Argentina. After Karl's performance against Ali, many felt he had a good chance to defeat Bonavena. Oscar though turned in a career best performance. He floored Karl in four different rounds, but the game Mildenberger made it to the final bell. Bonavena won a clear cut twelve round decision.

Karl would again defend his European title successfully against Gerhard Zech. What came then was a seventh round knockout loss to

Leotis Martin. On September 18, 1968, Mildenberger met Henry Cooper in London for the European crown. Karl lost the title to Cooper via a controversial disqualification for illegal use of the head. It would be Karl's last fight.

Mildenberger would retire with a fine 53-6-3 record. He recorded 19 knockouts while he was stopped on four occasions. He met five men who also challenged for the world title. Karl also held the European title nearly four years defending it six times.

MARTY MONROE

Back in the late 1970's and early 80's, there was a pretty good heavyweight out on the West Coast. His name was Marty Monroe. Marty was from Los Angeles, and he turned pro in 1974. In 1976 he beat another up and coming heavyweight named Randy Mack. In 1977 he defeated tough Joe Gholston. In 1978 he defeated Leroy Boone.

In 1980 Marty would lose a decision to the rough and rugged Scott Ledoux. Marty bounced right back with impressive stoppage victories over Lynn Ball and Eddie "The Animal" Lopez. Marty was now a force to be reckoned with.

In 1981 Monroe would meet the streaking Greg Page. At this time Page was considered one of the best heavyweight prospects in the game. Greg proved to be too much for Monroe halting a game Marty in the sixth round. That might have been the best performance in the career of Greg Page. Marty would lay off for two years and then return to win two fights. He ended his career in 1983 with a very respectable 25-2-1 record. He scored sixteen knockouts and was stopped only once.

RANDY NEUMANN

An overlooked heavyweight in the talent rich 1970's was New Jersey's Randy Neumann. Born on July 21, 1948, Randy joined the punch for pay ranks in 1969. He reeled off eleven straight wins, but in 1971, he was stopped in two by Jimmy Harris. Randy came right back to decision Harris in a return bout.

Randy continued his move up the ladder with two decisions over rugged Argentine Raul Gorosito and a verdict over Brian O'Melia. On December 9, 1971, Randy captured the New Jersey State heavyweight title by outscoring Chuck Wepner. In 1972 Randy followed the Wepner win with a points victory over Jimmy Young at Madison Square Garden. A month later he lost the New Jersey title back to Wepner.

In 1973 Randy received an opportunity to meet long time top contender Jerry Quarry who was beginning a comeback. Quarry proved to be too much, halting Randy after seven rounds. Neumann attempted to regain the New Jersey title in 1974 but lost in seven to Wepner.

Despite a disqualification loss in the Bahamas to Wendell Joseph, 1975 saw Randy score his biggest career victory as he out boxed Boone Kirkman over ten rounds. The win gave Randy another date at the Garden this time against unbeaten prospect Duane Bobick. The hard-hitting Bobick floored Randy three times in the fourth round for an automatic TKO.

Randy had his last fight in 1977 when he was taken out in five rounds by Ibar Arrington. In all, Neumann had 38 bouts, winning 31 of them. He scored 11 knockouts. Of his seven losses, he was stopped five times. Randy was a smart and smooth boxer, but he lacked the big punch. He also had a tendency to cut. He was a game battler though, and he always came to fight. Today he is one of the most respected referees in the business.

KEN NORTON

When there is any talk of the greatest era of heavyweight boxing, the name Ken Norton has to be mentioned. Ken was a mainstay in the ratings throughout the 1970's, and he briefly wore the World Boxing Council version of the heavyweight title. Norton, of course, is remembered most for his famous trilogy with Muhammad Ali.

Norton was born on August 9, 1943, in Jacksonville, Illinois. He was always an exceptional athlete but didn't turn to boxing until he joined the Marine Corp. He won the All Marine heavyweight championship three times and compiled a 24-2 amateur record. After being passed over to represent the United States in the Pan American Games, Ken opted to turn professional. He made his debut on November 14, 1967, by halting Grady Brazell in the fifth round in San Diego. It would be the first of sixteen straight victories for Ken. During the streak, Norton would gain experience beating veterans like Bill McMurray and Aaron Eastling.

It would all come crashing down on July 2, 1970, at the Olympic Auditorium in Los Angeles. Norton would meet a lanky heavyweight from Venezuela named Jose Luis Garcia. Based on appearance, it looked like the muscular Norton would steamroll his opponent. Garcia, though, possessed fast hands, and he could bang. In a major upset, Garcia took out Ken in the eighth round. It was back to the drawing board for Norton.

Ken would begin to see a hypnotist, and this seemed to work as he rallied to win thirteen straight contests. Norton moved up the heavyweight rankings with two wins over the capable James J. Woody. He defeated rugged Jack O'Halloran in a thriller and stopped the talented Henry Clark. On March 31, 1973, Ken would meet former heavyweight champion Muhammad Ali in San Diego. Ali had failed to regain the heavyweight title on March 8, 1971, against Joe Frazier in the "Fight Of The Century". Ali was now taking on all comers to establish himself as the "People's Champion" and entice Frazier into a rematch. Norton was viewed as just another opponent, and Ali was listed as a 5 to 1 favorite. Ken hadn't read the script though, and he came out and forced the fight. Ali suffered a broken jaw in one of the early rounds, but he gamely fought on. This day Ken was too much for Muhammad, and Norton was awarded a well-deserved decision. Along with it came the North American Boxing Federation heavyweight title.

Ali and Norton would meet again on September 10, 1973, at the Inglewood Forum. Ali vowed to be in better shape, and he was.

Muhammad swept the early rounds, but as the bout progressed, Norton came on strong. At the end of twelve rounds, Ali's early lead held up, and he won the verdict. After giving "The Greatest" twelve rounds of pure hell, Ken was given a shot at the heavyweight title. The man in the other corner would be undefeated George Foreman. The power punching Foreman had destroyed Joe Frazier in two rounds to capture the title. At this point in his career George looked unbeatable. The fight would take place March 26, 1974, in Caracas, Venezuela. After a quiet first round George would lower the boom in round two. Again it was back to the drawing board for Ken.

The two fights with Ali still left Norton as a very marketable heavyweight. Ken came back with a vengeance. He took apart Boone Kirkman, and then in 1975, he scored knock out wins over Jerry Quarry and former conqueror Garcia. In 1976 he had inside the distance wins over Pedro Lovell, Ron Stander and Larry Middleton. In 1974 Ali upset Foreman in the famous "Rumble In The Jungle" to regain the championship. Now Ken was considered the #1 threat to his title. Their rubber match took place on September 28, 1976, at Yankee Stadium. After fifteen see saw rounds, Ali was given a highly controversial decision to retain his crown. Norton was heartbroken, but he vowed to get Ali one more time.

In 1977 Ken reinforced his status as the number one contender by demolishing unbeaten Duane Bobick in one round. Later in the year he met the crafty Jimmy Young in a World Boxing Council heavyweight eliminator. The fight with Young took place on November 5, 1977, in Las Vegas. In an extremely close affair, Norton edged Young, and Ken was now Ali's mandatory challenger. In 1978 a fading Ali would lose his title to unbeaten but untested Leon Spinks in a huge upset. Spinks was now obligated to defend the title against Norton. Leon, though, would opt for a much more lucrative rematch with Ali. The WBC then stripped Spinks of the title and awarded it to Norton based on his win over Young. Finally Norton was a champion.

Ken's tenure as champion was short lived. On June 9, 1978, in Las Vegas, Norton would lose a razor close verdict to unbeaten Larry Holmes in a truly classic battle. Ken would fight on hoping for another crack at the title. He stopped classy Randy Stephens in three rounds. Then disaster struck in the form of Earnie Shavers powerful fists. Shavers blasted Norton out in one round derailing any hopes of a Holmes rematch. Next Ken took on rough and tumble Scott LeDoux. Norton was winning handily but faded after taking a thumb to the eye. Norton was knocked down twice in the tenth and final round but hung on until the bell. The fight ended in a draw. Ken would retire but then come back a year later to face undefeated Randall "Tex" Cobb. Norton was able to out box the plodding Cobb and win the decision. Next for Norton would be the unbeaten punching sensation Gerry Cooney. There was already a great demand for Cooney to meet champion Larry Holmes. Norton would supply Gerry with his toughest test to date. The test ended in the first round as Cooney scored a brutal knock out. That ended the career of Ken Norton.

In all, Norton had fifty professional fights. His record was a very respectable 42-7-1. Ken scored thirty three knockouts and was stopped four times. He met three champions in Ali, Foreman and Holmes. He also faced eight boxers who challenged for the title. He was among the elite heavyweights for nearly a decade.

JACK O'HALLORAN

As Muhammad Ali ruled the heavyweight division in the mid 1960's, white hope contenders came and went. Henry Cooper, George Chuvalo and Karl Mildenberger all were vanquished by the "Greatest". When Ali was forced to relinquish his crown in 1967, the best of the white contenders was probably Jerry Quarry. By 1969 a huge brute of a man named Jack O'Halloran had compiled an impressive 16-1-1 record. Standing at around 6'6" and weighing in the vicinity of 240 pounds, Jack struck fear into opponents by his mere bulk. In 1969 he upgraded his opposition with mixed results. He dropped decisions to Joe "King" Roman, Joe Bugner and

Tony Doyle. On August 19th he was halted by rugged "Florida" Al Jones. In turn he outscored Carl Gizzi and stopped Mexican contender Manuel Ramos in seven rounds.

On January 26th, 1970, in New York O'Halloran was kayoed by George Foreman in five rounds. On April 9th he was destroyed in one round by Mac Foster. Jack lost a rematch with Roman, but he did manage to outpoint British Danny McAliden. 1971 was a dismal year for O'Halloran as he lost to Jack Bodell, John Griffin, Ron Stander and Ron Lyle. Jack did decision the still dangerous Cleveland Williams, and he kayoed Terry Daniels.

Big Jack made his move in 1972 as he fought his way into the heavyweight ratings. On March 17th he lost a ten round donnybrook to future champion Kenny Norton. Many felt this was one of the best bouts between big men on the west coast in years. On June 16th Jack dropped a verdict to a highly regarded Henry Clark. On August 10th in what became Jack's career highlight victory, he won a twelve round rematch with Clark for the California State heavyweight title. One month later he halted Ali's brother Rudy Clay (Rahman Ali) in eight rounds. Quickly Jack put out a challenge to Muhammad to avenge his brother's loss. Luckily for Jack the ex-champ had other commitments.

Jack started 1973 where he left off in 1972. He pounded out a ten round decision over Al "Blue" Lewis. He then split a pair of knockouts with Jimmy Summerville. On June 8th Jack lost the California State title to Howard "Kayo" Smith via a twelve round points call. Jack then dropped back to back verdicts to Boone Kirkiman and Koli Vailee. On December 5th O'Halloran was stopped in nine rounds by Larry Middleton. That loss pretty much finished Jack as a viable contender. In all Jack fought two world champions and seven others challenged for the crown. Also include top contenders such as Al Jones, Al Lewis, Mac Foster, Henry Clark, Boone Kirkman and Larry Middleton, and you can see Jack did battle with the cream of the crop.

JOEY ORBILLO

During the 60's and the early 1970's the state of California produced several world class heavyweights, talented and capable boxers like Eddie Machen, Jerry Quarry, Henry Clark, Bill McMurray, Mac Foster, Howard "Kayo" Smith and Kenny Norton.

The city of Wilmington was represented by a rough and tough customer by the name of Joey Orbillo. Joey did not have a lot of fights in a career that lasted less than a decade. He did have a lot of memorable wars. He was a game and brawling crowd pleaser. If it was blood and guts you wanted, Joey gave it to you.

He began his career in the mid-1960's and was soon swapping leather with the likes of Henry Clark, Johnny Featherman and future world title challenger Manuel Ramos. Joey scored a big victory in March of 1966 outscoring the highly regarded Tony Doyle. At the time Doyle was hot. The win over Doyle set the stage for Joey to invade the top layer of the heavyweight division. He was matched with Eddie Machen. The veteran was among the best in the world. On June 23, 1966, he proved to be a little too much for Joey winning a hotly contested ten round split decision.

Orbillo put up such a fine showing against Machen that he was then matched with the streaking Jerry Quarry. This bout was a matchmaker's dream, and it lived up to all expectations. The aggressive Orbillo forced the action, and the slick Quarry counterpunched beautifully. In the fourth round, Quarry stunned Orbillo with a counter hook off the ropes. Jerry then followed with a series of ripping brain jarring shots that dropped Orbillo. How Joey got up from this knockdown and still fought on was a testament to his sheer guts and will. Veteran trainer Gil Clancy, who handled Quarry later in his career, called Jerry the hardest puncher he ever had. Gil had once trained George Foreman! Quarry won the decision, but Joey's gameness won the crowd.

Joey's career slowed down after the loss to Quarry. He had a couple of wins over journeyman Roy "Cookie" Wallace. Then in 1968 he lost to

Amos "Big Train" Lincoln. Finally on November 18, 1971, Orbillo was halted in five rounds by Roby Harris.

Orbillo has pretty much been forgotten, but anyone who saw his war with Quarry will never forget him.

GREGORIO PERALTA

Sometimes it isn't just talent that makes someone successful inside the ropes. A generous dash of luck usually helps. Also being in the right place at the right time doesn't hurt. Unfortunately for Gregorio Peralta of Argentina, on this occasion two out of three isn't good. He had talent and lots of it, but he lacked luck and the ability to be in the right place. Peralta was a throwback to the cagey old veteran boxers of decades before. He campaigned successfully in two weight divisions throughout the sixties and early seventies. As a light heavyweight, he carried a pretty solid wallop to go along with his uncanny ring generalship. He defeated champion Willie Pastrano in a non-title bout to qualify for a 1964 title shot. Pastrano fought maybe the best fight of his career, but Peralta stayed right with him until a cut forced a stoppage in Willie's favor. Gregorio would never receive another attempt at a championship.

Gregorio at this time held the Argentine heavyweight title. He decided to campaign strictly as a heavyweight. He outpointed Roberto Davila retaining the South American heavyweight championship only three months after losing to Pastrano. Then Peralta lost a twelve round decision to fellow countryman Oscar Bonevena in September of 1965 prompting a twenty month layoff. Returning in 1967 Gregorio won 26 of 29 fights with only draws against Chuck Leslie, Vittorio Saraudi and Bonevena marring the streak. In 1969 plans were being made for Peralta to challenge World Boxing Association heavyweight champion Jimmy Ellis in Buenos Aries. Ellis was on a collision course with Joe Frazier, and he wanted to make a defense of his title before his showdown with "Smokin' Joe". For whatever reasons, the proposed Ellis-Peralta bout fell through. Ellis went on to fight Frazier and lose. On the undercard of Frazier-Ellis, Peralta met 1968 Olympic Gold Medalist George Foreman. This was probably Gregorio's shining moment. Taking everything a still green but powerful Foreman could offer, Peralta stayed in the bout with an exhibition of guile and guts. Peralta lost a tough decision to George, but he won over the Madison Square Garden crowd with his performance.

In 1971, Foreman finally caught up to Gregorio in the tenth round of their rematch to score a knockout. Peralta then went on a successful tour of Europe in which he scored an important kayo victory over Jose Urtain. On August 1, 1972, in Barcelona, Spain, Gregorio met Muhammad Ali in an eight round exhibition bout giving a good account of himself. In 1973 Peralta twice fought the dangerous Ron Lyle losing a decision in Denver and then holding Lyle to a draw in Frankfurt, Germany. Eventually Gregorio faded into retirement.

I wonder how Peralta would have made out if he would have met Ellis in front of thousands of cheering countrymen. Whenever anyone mentions great heavyweights from Argentina, you're sure to hear Luis Firpo and Bonevena. Please don't forget a fine fighting machine named Gregorio Peralta.

JERRY QUARRY

Remember Jerry Quarry? He was a perennial mainstay in the heavyweight division throughout the1960's and 1970's. The dominant "White Hope" of that era, Jerry was always in the thick of the title picture and had a tremendous following. The fans either loved him or hated him. They could never seem to find a middle ground and neither could the odds makers. Just when it seemed that Quarry had arrived at the crest of his skills, those skills would desert him. Untimely losses and remarkable comeback wins were his claim to fame. What Jerry had is what many of today's top heavyweights lack. That was charisma. Win or lose the fans always got their money's worth and the press produced reams of copy on Jerry's adventures in and out of the ring.

Quarry entered the pro ranks with the reputation as a comer. An accomplished amateur, Jerry's progress up the fistic ladder was on its way. As Jerry began to establish his credentials he began to receive more and more interest. One of the interested parties was the none other than Rocky Marciano. The rumor was that the "The Rock" was willing to pay $100,000 for Jerry's contract, big money in those days. Just as this rosy scenario was unfolding the fates sent Jerry an omen of things to come. Their messenger was Eddie Machen. Eddie was a hard luck ex-contender on the way down the ladder. His name would look good on Quarry's resume. Fittingly when they entered Machen's name on Jerry's record, there was an L-10 next to it. Marciano was no longer interested in Jerry's contract and now Quarry, with dogged determination that he would show throughout his career, began the rebuilding process.

During his career much was written about the relationship Jerry had with the "Quarry Clan". Managed by his father, Jack, and constantly surrounded by family members, the press could never figure if the "Clan" was good for Jerry or not. Jerry seemed to have the same problem with his unconditional loyalty, internal arguments and marital difficulties. The "Clan's" battle royales in the auditorium parking lots sometimes upstaged Jerry's fight. The press loved it, and the fans ate it up.

With or without family woes, Quarry's career was soon back on track. When he held former champion Floyd Patterson to a draw, he had hit the big time. Again the fates would take over. Muhammad Ali was forced from his throne for refusing to enter the United States Army. Quickly the World Boxing Association chose eight men to compete in an elimination tournament to determine Ali's successor. Jerry was one of the eight chosen. In his first tourney bout he was again pitted against Patterson. This time Jerry got the verdict. In his next match Quarry squared off against tournament favorite, Thad Spencer. Spencer had defeated ex-W.B.A. champ, Ernie Terrell and now the experts were picking him to beat Quarry. Jerry proved the experts wrong stopping Spencer in round twelve. Now Quarry was made the favorite in the championship match against Jimmy Ellis. Ellis was managed by Angelo Dundee and was a former spar mate of Ali's. Still the experts said that Ellis was just a blown up middleweight. They forgot that Ellis had beaten Leotis Martin and Oscar Bonavena to get to the finals. The bout itself was dull. Both men refused to lead, and the quicker handed Ellis won the decision and the title. Jerry's stock dropped dramatically, and many began to wonder if Jerry "had the goods."

Quarry's loss to Ellis brought Jerry and the "Clan" back to reality. It was again time to start over. Jerry wasted little time as he trounced Buster Mathis over twelve rounds. His reward was a shot at the New York State heavyweight crown held by none other than Joe Frazier. The first two rounds of Jerry's 1969 bout with Frazier may have been Jerry's finest. He outslugged the consummate slugger. Soon though, it became apparent that this was Frazier's kind of fight. Jerry faded and was stopped in seven. Later that year Quarry met another top white hope in George Chuvalo. For six rounds Quarry out boxed his plodding foe. Desperate and bleeding, Chuvalo came to life in round seven and floored Jerry. Quarry was dazed and misread the referee's count. The ref tolled ten, and Jerry was counted out.

Disbelieving and disillusioned, it looked to Jerry like he had reached the end. Trying to squeeze one more payday from the Quarry name, Madison Square Garden matched Jerry with Mac Foster who was 24-0 with 24 knockouts and the no. 1 contender. Again Jerry bounced back into the heavyweight picture destroying Foster in six rounds. Jerry's reward was a shot against the returning Muhammad Ali. Although Jerry fought well, a bad cut over his eye led to a third round stoppage. Quarry stayed active but the fire seemed to be missing. Not quite two years after their first bout, Jerry met Ali again. This time it was no contest. Ali dominated Jerry, and the bout was halted in round seven. His performance was lethargic, and the experts had written Jerry off as a has been. Deciding to give it one more try, Jerry hooked up with trainer Gil Clancy and began another remarkable comeback. A twelve round decision over previously unbeaten Ron Lyle put Jerry back in the ratings. He solidified this when he stopped Earnie Shavers in one round. Jerry was now matched for a second time again with Joe Frazier. Frazier-Quarry II was a mismatch. Jerry was never in the fight which was mercifully halted in round five. Jerry had one more shot at the big time when he was matched with Ken Norton. Game but out of condition, Quarry scored well early but ran out of gas. Norton picked him apart and stopped Jerry in the fifth. There was an awful come from behind victory over Lorenzo Zanon. Then Jerry slipped into oblivion. He later tried to return as a cruiserweight, but his skills had long ago eroded.

The post career problems that Jerry faced have been well documented. A testimony to every punch he absorbed from Ali, Frazier, and all the other top heavyweights he crossed gloves with. Who knows how Jerry's career would have gone if Ali and Frazier had not boxed in the same era? He has nothing to be ashamed of. He was a ranked contender for ten years in possibly the toughest heavyweight division of any era. When the division did become a little stagnant, you better bet Jerry would do something to stir it up.......charisma.

MANUEL RAMOS

When you think of Mexican fighters, it is usually a tough little hombre like a Ruben Olivares, Vincente Saldivar or Julio Cesar Chavez. More often than not the better battlers from Mexico scaled under 160lbs. In an exception to the rule during the mid-60 to the early 70's, this country produced a pretty fair heavyweight. He fought two world champions and nine others that challenged for the heavyweight crown. His name was Manuel Ramos. Although he lost more fights then he won, the names on his resume are quite impressive.

When Ramos made his way from Mexico to the West Coast, he quickly began meeting the best opposition available. In 1964 he lost a decision to Henry Clark and drew with Joey Orbillo. In 1965 he lost a rematch to Orbillo and drew with George "Scrap Iron" Johnson. He finished the year losing by a knockout to Lars Norling.

In 1966 Manuel began a win streak that would carry him to a world title shot. He knocked out Norling in a rematch and then stopped Archie Ray in eight. Next Manuel would outpoint faded ex-contender Eddie Machen. In 1967 Ramos halted James J. Woody in two, and then, on October 14th in Mexico City, he faced ex-World Boxing Association heavyweight champion Ernie Terrell. Manuel scored an upset ten round decision. Two victories in 1968 brought Manuel's streak to fifteen straight and set up a title fight with "Smokin" Joe Frazier. The bout took place June 24th at <u>Madison Square Garden</u>. Joe held the New York State heavyweight crown when he entered the ring, and two rounds later, he left with his crown intact. Joe overwhelmed Ramos in what would be Manuel's only shot. Three months later Manuel was taken apart by George Chuvalo in five rounds.

Ramos began to rebuild his career in 1969 by beating Tony Doyle, but Jack O'Halloran stopped him in his next bout. Manuel had seven bouts in 1970 and won only one of them. He lost to Chuck Wepner, Joe Bugner, Jimmy Richards and Joe "King" Roman. He drew with Ron Stander and was stopped in one round by Oscar "Ringo" Bonevena. Manuel had seven more bouts in 1971 and again won only one, losing to Jurgen Blin, Jack Bodell, Elmo Henderson, Terry Daniels, Stander and Ron Lyle.

In 1973 Ramos was halted in four by Johnny Hudgins. Then in 1973 he lost to Luis Pires and Armando Zanini. In his last chance at the big time, he faced Olympian Duane Bobick but was taken in seven rounds thus finishing him as a formidable heavyweight contender.

ALFIO RIGHETTI

Alfio Righetti turned pro in 1974 and won his first 21 bouts. Win #22 came in 1976 when he beat tough Bepi Ros. In his next fight, Righetti won the Italian heavyweight title defeating Dante Cane.

In 1977 Alfio lost a decision to up and coming Olympic Gold Medalist Leon Spinks. Righetti would then go on to win his next nine battles. In 1979 he met fellow countryman Lorenzo Zanon for the European championship. After twelve rounds, it was adjudged a draw, thus Zanon retained his title.

In his next fight, Righetti would meet Cleveland, Ohio, journeyman Terry Mims. In a major upset, Mims halted Righetti in round one. That was Alfio's last fight. His final record was 36-2-1 with 17 knockout victories.

On a side note, Terry Mims ended his career with a 13-16 record. He lost to the likes of Michael Dokes, Duane Bobick, Tex Cobb, Bernard Benton and Evander Holyfield. He also holds an upset victory over Leon Spinks.

EARNIE SHAVERS

Possibly the best heavyweight to ever come out of the state of Ohio was Earnie "The Acorn" Shavers. Born on August 31, 1945, in Alabama, his real name is Earnie Dee Shaver. He attended school in Warren, Ohio and made a name for himself as a football player. Earnie was just a great all-around athlete, and when the boxing bug bit him, he took to it like a duck to water.

What Earnie accomplished in boxing is phenomenal, but the world championship eluded him. Nevertheless in both of his failed attempts at the crown, he left an indelible mark in the memory of those who witnessed the bouts. Earnie became a professional boxer in 1969. He won his first two fights by KO and dropped a six rounder to Stan Johnson. Two fights later he stopped J.D. McCauley, the uncle of future champion James "Buster" Douglas. In 1970 Shavers suffered his second loss. He was halted by future world title challenger Ron Stander. Earnie would then run off a 32 fight win streak in which he kayoed 31 opponents. Only former WBA light heavyweight titleholder Vincente Rondon went the ten round route with him.

The streak led Earnie to his first shot at the big time. In June of 1973 Shavers met former World Boxing Association heavyweight champion Jimmy Ellis at Madison Square Garden. Jimmy was still a serious contender, and he was hoping for a win over the red hot Shavers that would put him back into the title picture. The fight started at a fast pace, and Jimmy appeared to have stunned Shavers. Ellis then went after Earnie. Out of nowhere Shavers unleashed an uppercut with KO written all over it. Down went Ellis in a semi-conscious condition, and he was counted out. Just like that it was over, and Earnie was an instant contender. Jimmy's astute manager Angelo Dundee said his guy got caught by a sucker punch. Whatever it was, Shavers was in the Top Ten.

In December Shavers returned to the Garden to face the highly ranked and enormously popular "Irish" Jerry Quarry. The winner could be in line to fight heavyweight champion George Foreman. This time the tables were turned on Earnie. Quarry hurt him early and did not let him off the hook. Finally the referee intervened to save Shavers. In less than two rounds Earnie's career had peaked and then collapsed. A 1974 loss to solid journeyman Bob Stallings made it appear that Shavers was just a flash in the pan. Later in 1974 Shavers drew with clever Jimmy Young. A fighter he had stopped in one round in 1972. Little did we know at that time how good Jimmy Young would become.

In 1975 Shavers met the dangerous Ron Lyle. This was one of the best heavyweight fights I've ever seen. Earnie had Lyle down early in the fight. Lyle arose right before the bell. He then proceeded to out punch Earnie in a classic slug fest. Finally Lyle pounded Shavers to the canvas like a man hammering a nail into a floor. It was over in round six. Surely Shavers was through. Earnie though embarked on a comeback that brought him back to the forefront of the heavyweight division. He beat the respected Henry Clark twice, the second time by a convincing knockout. He came from behind to halt the feared Roy "Tiger" Williams. He then halted Howard "Kayo" Smith in two. This led Earnie to a title shot against "The Greatest", Muhammad Ali. It was 1977 at the Garden, and Ali and Shavers put on a show. Several times during the bout Earnie's bombs rocked Ali to his very foundation. Still Ali was still Ali, and he sucked it up to outscore Shavers. In defeat, though, Earnie gained a legion of loyal fans.

In 1978 Shavers met upstart Larry Holmes. In this bout Holmes served notice that he was a future star. He out boxed and shut out Shavers over twelve rounds. Later Holmes would win the World Boxing Council version of the heavyweight title in an action packed fifteen rounder against Ken Norton. In 1979 Earnie met Norton in a title eliminator. Shavers eliminated Ken in one round. The Holmes – Shavers rematch took place later in 1979. The blueprint was the same as Larry out slicked Earnie. In round seven, though, lightning struck. Shavers hit Holmes with a punch that dropped him like he had been shot. I'll never know how Larry got up after being hit like that. He did though and ended up stopping a tired and bleeding Shavers in the eleventh.

From this point on, Earnie's career began to decline. He lost to Bernardo Mercado and Tex Cobb in 1980 but both felt the effects of Earnie's thunderous blows. In 1981 Shavers rebounded with a stoppage win over Jeff Sims. In 1982 Shavers took out the normally durable Joe Bugner in two rounds. That was Earnie's swan song. He would drop verdicts to James "Quick" Tillis and Walter Santemore. To the credit of Tillis, he gamely arose to fight on after Earnie nearly decapitated him. A 1983 disqualification loss to the under rated George Chaplin sent Earnie into retirement.

Shavers returned four years later and then again retired. Eight years later he made an ill-fated comeback. After being stopped in two rounds by Brian Yates, Earnie hung them up for good. In 89 bouts Shavers posted a sterling 74-14-1 record against the great heavyweights of the 1970's and 80's. He scored 68 KO's. He had a 76.4% KO percentage. His credentials earned him the distinction as the "puncher of the century"! Warranted? Ask Ali, Norton, Holmes, etc.... When he caught an opponent clean, they did the shimmy and shake. Watch his bouts with Norton, Howard Smith and the Henry Clark rematch. Oh the man could swing!

HOWARD SMITH

When a fighter earns the nickname "Kayo", it's safe to assume he's a pretty dangerous guy. Howard "Kayo" Smith met and defeated some top tier heavyweights in the 1970's. Yes, he could bang with the best of them.

Howard turned professional in 1971 and suffered a defeat in his fourth pro fight. He bounced right back in 1972 halting future world champion Mike Weaver in three rounds. Next he outscored Weaver in a return match. In 1973 Howard pounded out a decision over Jack "The Giant" O'Halloran. Smith was moving up in the heavyweight rankings in 1974 with KO wins over Tony Doyle and O'Halloran in a rematch. Howard leaped over another hurdle in 1975 with a fifth round stoppage of the respected Larry Middleton. In 1976 Smith won a split decision over the smooth boxing Johnny Boudreaux.

1977 proved to be a pivotal year for Howard. He solidified his Top Ten ranking by outscoring the clever Henry Clark. Then in April in Las Vegas, Howard met the hard belting Earnie Shavers. This was a much anticipated match between two of divisions premier punchers. Who would get in the first big shot? Well on this night it was the feared Shavers who dropped Howard three times in the first round. The bout was halted in the second round. It was a disappointing loss, but Smith returned to action four months later knocking out Charlie James in the tenth round. That would be Howard's last fight.

Smith only had twenty pro fights, (17-2-0 with 1 no contest). He won ten via the knockout route. In his brief career Smith made his mark in the talent rich heavyweight division of the 1970's.

RENALDO "MISTER" SNIPES

He came within an eyelash of upsetting the great Larry Holmes and winning the heavyweight championship of the world. For the better part of the 1980's, he was ranked in the top ten. By the time his career ended, he had crossed gloves with no less than eight men who at one time held the moniker, world champion.

Renaldo "Mister" Snipes was born on August 15, 1956, in Houston, Texas. He fought out of Yonkers, N.Y. as he turned pro in 1978. He won his first twenty two bouts, and he progressed quickly up in the rankings. In 1980, Snipes halted Larry Alexander and Dwain Bonds. In 1981, Snipes made his move. He defeated the powerful Floyd "Jumbo" Cummings. Then Snipes outscored light heavyweight champion Eddie Mustafa Muhammad. Snipes next met the hard punching Gerrie Coetzee. Snipes was awarded what I felt was a terrible decision over the South African.

The win over Coetzee enabled Snipes to get a shot at WBC titleholder Larry Holmes. The fight took place November 6, 1981, in Pittsburgh. Holmes was a heavy favorite, and he dominated most of the first six rounds. In round seven, though, Snipes connected with a bomb, and down went Holmes. Larry gamely got up, but he was in bad shape. Somehow Holmes would survive the round much like he did when Earnie Shavers had decked him in an earlier fight. Holmes regained control of the bout over the next few rounds. In the eleventh, Holmes hurt Snipes badly and was all over him forcing the referee to wave the fight off. Although Snipes was in trouble, it seemed a bit unfair to Snipes that the referee halted the contest. When Snipes had Holmes reeling after a knockdown, he allowed Holmes to go on.

Regardless of the loss to Holmes, Snipes stayed in the mix in 1982 drawing with rugged Scott Frank, losing a decision to "Terrible" Tim Witherspoon and then defeating Trevor Berbick. In 1983 he was defeated by Greg Page and Alfredo Evangelista. In 1984, Snipes was outpointed by future cruiser weight king Rickey Parkey. A 1986 loss to Olympian Tyrell Biggs pretty much pushed Renaldo out of any title fight consideration. In 1988, Snipes lost to another future cruiser weight champion in Orlin Norris.

Snipes would make one more attempt to resurrect his career as he put together a ten fight win streak that included a KO win over Johnny DuPlooy. Finally in 1993, Renaldo's career came to an end as he was soundly beaten and stopped by an up and coming Jorge Luis Gonzalez.

Renaldo finished his highly respectable career with 48 fights. His final ledger was 39-8-1. He scored 22 knockouts while he was only stopped twice, by Holmes and Gonzalez. That says a lot considering the competition he met. The eight champions he met were Holmes, Coetzee, Page, Witherspoon, Berbick, Norris, Parkey and Eddie Mustafa Muhammad. He also met three others that fought for the heavyweight title in Scott Frank, Evangelista and Biggs. Needless to say, Mr. Snipes traveled in some pretty fast company.

THAD SPENCER

At one time he was the most prominent heavyweight in the world except for the deposed Muhammad Ali and streaking Olympic Gold Medalist Joe Frazier. He was the favorite to win the hastily put together World Boxing Association elimination tourney that was set up to find a successor to the alleged draft dodger Ali. When he beat ex-WBA champion Ernie Terrell in the opening round of the tournament, he seemed like a sure bet in to capture the vacant crown. Where did it all go wrong? Why did fate deal this talented boxer such a cruel blow? If only Thad Spencer knew what the future held for him.

The 5'11' 200 pounds Spencer began his professional journey on May 3, 1960, with a third round knockout over Frankie Rowe. He racked up five more wins before losing a four round decision to Shirley Pembleton, surely not the stuff that legends are made of. Nevertheless Thad would reel off twelve straight victories. Among his victims were Jefferson Davis and Jimmy Fletcher. Then in 1963 Spencer was outpointed by clever Chuck Leslie. In 1964 Thad scored four straight knockouts including a fifth round stoppage of former world title challenger Tom McNeeley. Then disaster struck on December 14th when Thad was halted in nine rounds by Amos "Big Train" Lincoln.

In 1965 Spencer came back strongly avenging the 1963 loss to Chuck Leslie. He then outscored Billy Daniels and Roger Rischer. In a rematch with Lincoln, Thad was decisioned over ten rounds. After opening 1966 by again outpointing Leslie and Daniels, he traveled to England. There he produced a two round knockout over Jack Bodell and a points win over Brian London. Just as Thad was gaining momentum, he was upset in seven by spoiler Bill McMurray. Undaunted Thad closed out the year with the biggest win of his career, a ten round verdict over Doug Jones. Thad had finally hit the big time.

Spencer's star would shine its brightest in 1967. He derailed his former nemesis Amos Lincoln in eight rounds and thus gained entry into the WBA's eight-man elimination tournament. On August 5th at the Houston Astrodome, Spencer convincingly took apart ex-champion Ernie Terrell. Thad's impressive performance made him the odds on favorite to become the new titleholder. Enter Jerry Quarry. On February 3, 1968, Thad met Quarry in Oakland. Jerry had struggled to win a disputed decision over ex-heavyweight king Floyd Patterson in his tournament opener. Many felt Thad would move past Quarry and into the finals. As usual in his sensational and erratic career, Jerry did the unexpected. Quarry gave Thad a one sided beating that was mercifully stopped in the twelfth and final round. Spencer's star had now fallen. How far it would fall in such a short period of time amazed the boxing experts. Thad turned in one more credible performance. In his next fight Spencer took another jaunt to England to meet Leotis Martin. Leotis had lost to the eventual tournament winner Jimmy Ellis on the same day that Thad had whipped Terrell. On May 28, 1968, Spencer and Martin hooked up in what many say was one of the best heavyweight fights on British soil. When the smoke had cleared, Leotis had emerged as a ninth round kayo victor.

Almost six months after the Martin loss, Thad was invited back to England to meet their "Golden Boy", Billy Walker. When Spencer entered the ring, it was unbelievable. His once chiseled body was covered with flab. His reflexes and his timing were hideous. Walker was at best a glorified club fighter, but he belted Thad all over the ring until it was stopped in round six. From top contender to this in less than a year, the downward spiral to oblivion had begun. Six months later Spencer traveled to Fresno and was halted in one round by the touted Mac Foster. He tried a comeback in 1970 drawing with Charlie Reno and losing a ten round duke to Tony Doyle. Then Thad was bombed out in two by Jose Luis Garcia. In 1971 he dropped decisions to Ron Stander and Doyle again.

After his victory over Terrell in 1967 that had put him on the threshold of the heavyweight championship, Thad failed to win his next nine starts, eight losses and a draw. Five times he was knocked out. How could a fighter's fortunes change so dramatically? Such was the tragic demise of Thad Spencer.

LEON SPINKS

Former world heavyweight champion Leon Spinks has surely received his share of negative press over the years. Many consider him just a footnote in heavyweight history, the man to which Muhammad Ali "loaned" his title. Leon was much more than that, much more.

One should first look at his decorated amateur career. Before entering the professional ranks Leon racked up a stellar 178-7 record. He won the National A.A.U. light heavyweight championship three years in a row

(1974-76). He then captured the 1976 Olympic Gold Medal in 1976. He was more than ready for the pro ranks. He turned professional in 1977, and in his fourth fight, he took out seasoned veteran Pedro Agosto in one round. Two fights later he drew with rugged contender Scott LeDoux. In his next bout he upset undefeated Alfio Righetti.

One year and one month after turning pro Leon took his 6-0-1 record into a Las Vegas ring to meet the self-proclaimed "Greatest", Muhammad Ali for the heavyweight championship of the world. Few if any gave Leon a chance. The Spinks camp claimed Ali was the greatest but Leon was the latest. It turned out that the Spinks camp was right. An ill prepared Ali was lethargic throughout the fifteen round contest. Spinks piled up points on sheer energy and aggression. At the final bell the hand of Leon Spinks was raised.

By beating Ali, Spinks was to next face the World Boxing Council's #1 contender Ken Norton. Spinks would instead take a much more lucrative rematch against Ali in a bout blessed by the World Boxing Association. The W.B.C. stripped Spinks of the title and recognized Norton as their champion. Regardless of the politics the Ali - Spinks rematch took place seven months later in New Orleans. This time a better conditioned Ali schooled Spinks over fifteen rounds. It marked the third time Ali had won the title making him the first to ever do it. Before the rematch Leon broke training camp on several occasions. His new found fame and love of the night life earned him the nickname "Neon Leon".

Spinks was now an ex-champion and Ali promptly retired. The W.B.A. set up a four man elimination tournament to determine Ali's successor. John Tate would knock out Kallie Knoetzee to advance, and Leon would meet Gerrie Coetzee. Leon's hopes of regaining the crown were dashed in less than a round by the hard punching Coetzee. For Spinks it was back to the drawing board. Leon put together a knockout over Alfredo Evangelista, a draw with Eddie "The Animal" Lopez and knockouts over Kevin Isaac and Bernardo Mercado. Leon was then awarded a crack at the W.B.C. titleholder Larry Holmes. The talented Holmes had won the title from

Norton, and on June 12, 1981, in Detroit he defended against Spinks. Leon was game, and he tried hard but was just outclassed by Holmes who stopped him in the third round.

Spinks decided to move down in weight and try the cruiserweight division in 1982. He beat Ivy Brown and then defeated the classy Jesse Burnett for the North American Boxing Federation cruiserweight title. In his next bout he met former world cruiserweight champion Carlos DeLeon. Leon was battered and stopped in the sixth round. In 1985 Spinks returned to the heavyweight division and reeled of five straight wins including a knockout over Kip Kane for the W.B.C. Continental Heavyweight title.

In 1986 Spinks was offered a shot at Dwight Muhammad Qawi's W.B.A. cruiserweight title. On March 22nd in Reno, Nevada, Leon was savaged in six rounds by Qawi. Returning to the heavyweight division Spinks was stopped by tough Rocky Sekorski. In 1987 Leon was blitzed in one round by the capable Jose Ribalta. Then there were more losses to Angelo Musone, Ladislao Mijangos and Cleveland's Terry Mims. On March 18, 1988, Spinks received his last shot at the big time. He took on ranked contender Randy "Tex" Cobb. It turned out to be a spirited effort by Leon but after ten rounds Cobb won a well-deserved decision in an entertaining fight. In his next fight Leon would lose in 33 seconds to journeyman Tony Morrison.

Spinks would take three years off, and on returning he put together a modest five bout win streak. He then lost to Kevin Porter. Leon would only win three of his last seven fights before hanging up the gloves in 1995. In a 46 bout career Spinks would end up with a 26-17-3 record. He scored 14 knockouts, and he was stopped on 9 occasions. Leon had the tools, and if he would have stayed a light heavyweight in the professional ranks, he may have carved out a great career. The heavyweights were where the money was at though. Throughout his career Spinks was his own worst enemy, but no one can take away the fact the he was once heavyweight champion of the whole wide world. It's in the books forever.

BIG JOHN TATE

He was to be the heir apparent to the retired Muhammad Ali. He was a big strong heavyweight who could box. Yes, Larry Holmes was the holder of the World Boxing Council's version of the heavyweight title. Larry had been embarrassed, though, in the amateurs by Duane Bobick. Yes, as a pro, he was undefeated. He beat an aging, slow and ponderous Earnie Shavers to qualify for a shot at the WBC title. Larry then defeated Ken Norton to win the vacant World Boxing Council championship. Still many thought of Larry as nothing more than Ali's sparring partner who was in the right place at the right time.

Enter Big John Tate...John was born in 1955, and he had a very successful amateur career although he was stopped in the Olympics by the great Teofilo Stevenson. He had a good pro style, and he quickly began to move up in the ratings after turning professional in 1977. In his fourth bout he outscored rugged Walter Santemore who would meet world champions Tony Tucker, Bonecrusher Smith, Trevor Berbick and Frank Bruno during his career. John would then win a close decision over Eddie "The Animal" Lopez. John was surely not being spoon fed opposition.

John made his move in 1978 with knockouts over Raul Gorosito, Bernardo Mercado and Santemore in a rematch. He then won a close decision over Johnny Boudreaux earning himself a rating. In 1979 Tate met the still highly regarded Duane Bobick and blasted him out in less than a round. John was then matched with power punching South African Kallie Knoetze in an eliminator by the World Boxing Association to determine a successor to the retired Muhammad Ali. The winner of Tate-Knoetze would meet the winner of a bout between another South African Gerrie Coetzee and former world champion Leon Spinks. Big John proved to be too much for Knoetze winning in eight rounds. Coetzee then sent Leon to the showers in a single round. Tate then met Coetzee in front of over 80,000 South African fans. John boxed and punched his way to a comfortable fifteen round decision over Coetzee and was now proclaimed the new W.B.A. champion.

There was now talk of Ali returning to fight Tate in a quest to win the championship for a fourth time. All John had to do was defeat Mike Weaver in a defense in front a fan friendly crowd in Knoxville, Tennessee. Weaver had given W.B.C. champion Larry Holmes a very tough fight at Madison Square Garden the year before. He would be considered a good measuring opponent to determine the difference between Holmes and Tate. After fourteen rounds John had a comfortable lead. All he had to do was last the fifteenth and final round. John was still there two minutes into the round. Just one more minute...one more minute...then it happened, a punch for the ages. Upon its impact John fell face first to the canvas, OUT COLD!

John was now an ex-champion. The possible Ali fight was gone. A unification bout with Holmes or a Coetzee rematch went up in smoke. Tate would take on Canadian Trevor Berbick in an attempt to resurrect his career. Berbick did not read the script as he sent John to the mat in round nine. In a span of less than three months, John had twice found himself helpless on the canvas. His career was now in shambles.

Eight months later John returned with a decision over Harvey Steichen. He scored a few meaningless knockouts, and then he had to travel the distance to defeat veterans Leroy Caldwell and Leroy Boone. A decision over Donnie Long led to a KO over Marty Capasso. John would not box again for almost three years.

When John reappeared, he weighed a whopping 274 pounds as he blitzed Steve Eisenbarth in a round. Tate scaled 293 when he won a decision over Calvin Jones. In 1988 John took his fourteen bout win streak to England to meet Noel Quarless. John trimmed down to 281, but Quarless won a ten round verdict. That was all for Tate's tenure as an active boxer.

John retired with a respectable 34-3 record with 23 knockouts, but I'll always think of him with the question, "What if?" Where would his career have gone if he could have just survived that final round against Weaver... just one more minute.

ERNIE TERRELL; A GIANT IN THE SHADOW OF ALI

Who was the second best heavyweight around during the first title reign of Muhammad Ali? A strong argument could be made for Chicago's Ernie Terrell. Why? Because he earned it, he was even good enough to hold the WBA version of the heavyweight title, but everyone knew who the "real" champ was.

Terrell turned professional in 1957. At 6'6" he learned early how to use his height and reach to his advantage. He developed a good jab and learned how to tie up his opponents on the inside. It wasn't pretty, but it was effective. He won eighteen of his first twenty contests losing two eight round split decisions to Johnny Gray. In 1960 he was outscored by the capable Wayne Bethea. In 1962 Ernie suffered a major setback when he was halted by the powerful Cleveland Williams.

Terrell began his march to the top in 1963 defeating Williams in a return match and top contender Zora Folley. In 1964 Big Ernie beat Gerhard Zech, Jefferson Davis and stopped a young Bob Foster. When the WBA stripped Ali of his title recognition, they matched Terrell with perennial contender Eddie Machen. It was an ugly fight with a lot of wrestling and little punching, but Terrell did what he had to do to win the "vacant" title.

Maybe Ernie was not considered the real champion, but he did establish himself as the most formidable challenger to Ali. He closed 1965 with a decision over rugged George Chuvalo. In 1966 Terrell defeated slick Doug Jones. Finally after a failed attempt, Terrell and Ali were finally matched to unify the title. The bout would take place at the Houston Astrodome. Ernie's bold refusal to acknowledge Ali's Muslim name and refer to him as Clay irked Muhammad who vowed to punish Ernie. Punish he did as Ali worked Terrell over throughout the fifteen rounder. Round after round Ali would lash out at Terrell with punishing jabs and flurries while screaming "what's my name?". To Ernie's credit, he gamely absorbed the punishment with a very swollen eye. When it was all over, there was no doubt who was the King of the heavyweights.

The WBA would later strip Ali of the title again in 1967 for refusing induction into the Armed Forces. An eight man elimination tourney was set up to determine Ali's successor. Ernie was one of the eight contestants and an early favorite to win the tournament. Terrell was eliminated in the first leg of the tourney being upset by Thad Spencer. Terrell looked to be finished when he next lost to Mexican Manuel Ramos. He would not fight again until 1970, and his comeback drew little interest until he scored a major upset in 1972 by halting highly rated Jose Luis Garcia. In 1973 Ernie lost a very controversial verdict to Chuck Wepner, but his career then came crashing down when he was belted out in one round by Jeff "Candy Slim" Merritt.

In all, Terrell fought 54 times winning 45 of them. He stopped 21 foes. Ernie suffered nine losses but was only stopped twice. Today Ernie is remembered as a footnote to Ali's pre-exile days. In reality he was a viable contender who was overshadowed by "The Greatest".

JOSE MANUEL IBAR URTAIN

Jose Manuel Ibar Urtain was a major player in the heavyweight title picture in the early 1970's. The native of Spain turned pro in 1968. He was the rage in Europe winning his first 30 fights by knockout including a win over Peter Weiland to capture the European heavyweight title. Finally rugged German Jurgen Blin took Urtain the fifteen round route but lost the verdict. Urtain's first loss was by a low blow disqualification to Alfredo Vogrig.

On November 10, 1970, Urtain met the ever popular Brit Henry Cooper in London. The wily Cooper withstood Urtain's early aggression and then used his masterful left hook to halt Urtain in the ninth. Urtain was extremely strong, but his boxing limitations were now exposed.

In 1971, Urtain was held to a draw by veteran journeyman Mariano Echevarria. In his next fight, Jose was stopped by the clever Gregorio Peralta. To his credit, Urtain came back to regain the European title by blasting out Jack Bodell in two rounds.

In 1972 Urtain was out slicked by the clever Joe "King" Roman over ten rounds. The "King" used this win as a springboard to getting a 1973 title shot against George Foreman. That ended in one disastrous round for Roman. Next, Urtain would lose his European title in a rematch with Jurgen Blin.

Urtain would come back and beat former World Boxing Association light heavyweight champion Vincente Rondon. Jose then drew in a rematch with Roman and scores a KO over Richard Dunn. Urtain would then be stopped by Rocky Campbell and Alberto Lovell. Those losses pretty much ended Urtain's run as a viable contender.

Alfredo Evangelista became Spain's #1 heavyweight taking Urtain out in 1976. In his last shot at glory in 1977, Urtain met Jean Pierre Coopman for the vacant European title. It was over in four rounds and so was Urtain's career.

Jose ended up with a respectable record of 56-11-4. He had 42 stoppage victories. I have the tape of his loss to Henry Cooper. Although outclassed in the end by the clever Cooper, Urtain was better than I expected. I do believe, with high profile trainers and quality sparring partners, he could have gone to another level. The best comparison I can make is that he was an Oscar Bonavena in the rough. Too bad he never got the polish that he needed.

BILLY WALKER

During the 1960's the fans were quite stirred by the prospects of a young heavyweight named Billy Walker. He was dubbed the "Blond Bomber" but later, because of drawing power, he was called the "Golden Boy". After winning the British amateur title at the age of 22, Walker was enticed to turn pro by a $25,000 signing bonus. He headlined in his first professional fight which took place on March 27, 1962. Walker received $9,000 for the contest he won by KO. That was serious money at that time. Walker drew so many fans, and because of this he never fought a preliminary fight.

In his first dozen bouts Billy went 10-1-1. In his twelfth bout he stopped another heavyweight prospect named Johnny Prescott. In a rematch Walker was on the losing end of a decision. In 1964 Walker won by disqualification against the seasoned Joe Bygraves. Walker was then surprisingly halted by American Bill Nielsen. Walker turned the tables in a return match taking Nielsen out in two rounds. Billy finished 1964 with a point's verdict over rugged Joe Erskine. Walker was inching his way up the British ratings.

In 1965 he stopped American Charley Powell in two. Then came a ten round decision loss to the gritty Brian London. Next Billy drew with Argentina's Eduardo Corletti. In a return go Corletti stopped Walker in the eighth round. This was a major setback for Walker, but he came back to win six straight. The win streak earned Walker a 1967 shot at Germany's Karl Mildenberger and the European heavyweight title. The southpaw Mildenberger proved to be too much for Walker as he retained his crown via an eighth round stoppage. In his next battle Billy drew the ever popular Henry Cooper. This would be for Cooper's British and Commonwealth heavyweight titles. Cooper held on to his belts halting Walker in six. In 1968 Walker rekindled the hopes of his fans as he clubbed his way to a TKO victory over the once highly regarded American Thad Spencer. In 1967 as part of the elimination tourney set up by the World Boxing Association to replace Muhammad Ali as champion; Spencer upset former WBA titlist Ernie Terrell. In Spencer's next fight he was eliminated by Jerry Quarry. Then Spencer engaged in a war with the crafty Leotis Martin. Thad lost in the ninth round. Still the win over Spencer looked good on Walker's record. It would be Billy's last victory.

In March of 1969 Walker suffered a TKO loss to Jack Bodell. That would be Walker's final fight. In all Walker engaged in 31 bouts. His record was a respectable 21-8-2. He recorded 16 stoppage victories. He was stopped on five occasions. He enjoyed tremendous popularity during his tenure as a boxer. He was the "Golden Boy".

STAN WARD

He crossed gloves with three world champions and did battle with several top contenders. In the mid and late 1970's he was considered one of the best young heavyweights in the world. Stan Ward would, for the better part of five years, be in and out of the heavyweight top ten, but never receive a title shot. For all of his hulking size, Stan lacked two important assets needed to compete with the top echelon heavyweights. He lacked the big punch and a solid chin.

Stan turned pro in 1974 and quickly established himself as a heavyweight with promise. In 1975 he fought draws with Johnny Boudreaux and Pat Duncan. In 1976 Stan entered the world ratings with a decision over Mac Foster and a stunning knock out over Jeff Merritt.

On September 14, 1977, Stan met rugged Ron Lyle in Las Vegas. After ten grueling rounds, Lyle was awarded the decision. After Stan's game showing against Lyle, he returned to California and outscored future champion Mike Weaver. In his next fight, clever Randy Stephens upset Stan. As Ward entered 1979, his record stood at 10-2-2, and it looked as if he was going to be a mainstay in the talent rich ratings. All that came crashing down in his next bout, a rematch with Mike Weaver. The murderous punching Weaver halted Stan in the ninth round and sent Ward's career reeling.

It would be over a year before Stan got back into the ring, but he quickly added three bouts to his win column. On February 7, 1981, Stan met Greg Page in Atlantic City. Most remember Greg as an out of shape ex-champion. At one time, though, Greg was a very good boxer. If you ever get the chance, watch a tape of Greg's bouts with Scott Ledoux and Marty Monroe. Then you will see what I mean. At that time Page was awesome! He would also prove to be too much for Stan halting him in the seventh round.

The loss to Page was really the beginning of the end for Stan. He would get his share of wins, but in the important matches, his chin would betray him. In 1982 Gerrie Coetzee stopped him in two rounds. In 1983

Mike Weaver again halted him in nine rounds. Stan had one bout in 1984 and was inactive in 1985. In 1986 he was stopped again, this time by Larry Alexander in two rounds. Stan would take off over three years, and when he returned, he scored a couple of insignificant wins and faded from the scene.

MIKE WEAVER

If I were to tell you there was once a heavyweight who lost his first professional fight by knockout, that this heavyweight would actually lose half of his first dozen fights, and if I told you he would go on to win a piece of the heavyweight crown and be a major player in the division for well over a decade, would you believe me?

Well this is a true Cinderella story. It is the career of former WBA heavyweight titleholder Mike "Hercules" Weaver, who, in my opinion, for nearly a five year period was the second best heavyweight in the world.

Mike turned pro in 1972, and he was matched tough from the very beginning. He lost his debut by knockout to future contender Howard "Kayo" Smith. He would then lose a five round decision to Smith in a rematch. Undefeated Billy Ryan would halt him in two rounds, and four fights later, unbeaten Larry Frazier would stop Mike in the second. In 1974 Weaver would drop a ten round duke to the much bigger Rodney Bobick. Then Mike would be taken out in seven by the streaking Olympian prospect Duane Bobick.

At this point the future of Mike Weaver looked very bleak. Over the next three and a half years, though, Weaver would put together a fairly impressive eight fight win streak. Among his victims were Tony Doyle, Jody Ballard, Dwain Bonds and hard hitting Pedro Lovell. This put Mike into a fight with the talented Stan Ward for the California heavyweight title. Ward outweighed Weaver by forty pounds and took a twelve round verdict. Seven months later Weaver was matched with Big Leroy Jones for the vacant North American Boxing Federation heavyweight title. Jones outweighed Mike by a whopping sixty- six pounds! Jones boxed his way to a twelve round decision over Weaver to capture the crown.

The determined Weaver would resurge his career by reeling off five straight wins in impressive fashion. He took out the very dangerous Bernardo Mercado in five rounds. He then met Stan Ward in a rematch. The vacant United States Boxing Association heavyweight title was on the line. This time Mike took care of Ward in the ninth round and put himself in a position for a shot at the world's heavyweight title.

On January 22, 1979, Weaver met World Boxing Council heavyweight titleholder Larry Holmes at New York's Madison Square Garden. Although Larry only held a piece of the title, he was widely regarded as the world's best heavyweight. Holmes brought in a glossy but well-earned 30-0 record into the Garden that night to meet the decided underdog Mike Weaver. Oh what a fight it was!

The superb Holmes jab would set the early pace, but at times Weaver would surprise Larry with a good jab of his own. Someone must have forgotten to tell Weaver he was a big underdog, because he sure was not fighting like one. As the bout progressed, Mike started to carry the fight to Holmes. On several occasions Weaver would rock Larry with powerful lefts to the head and body. These were hurtful punches by the challenger, but the ever proud Holmes kept the pace. Still the crowd was starting to sense an upset may be in the making. After ten well contested and brutal rounds, Holmes was ahead on the cards. Nevertheless, he looked the worse for wear as Weaver seemed to be coming on. Then came the pivotal eleventh round. Weaver was going like gangbusters now, and he was really working Larry over. The game champion was winging back, but he looked hurt and drained as his title seemed to be slipping away. Toward the end of the round, Weaver was hammering Holmes in a corner. Then out of nowhere, Larry landed a huge uppercut that sent Weaver down against the ropes. It was obvious that Mike was badly shaken, as he barely pulled himself up by the ropes. Holmes followed up quickly, but time ran out. As the fighters came out for round twelve, it was plain to see that Weaver was still on queer street. Holmes jumped all over him, and soon the referee was forced to halt the fight. Larry had won the war, but Weaver had won the fans.

Mike Weaver was now a proven commodity. Later in 1979 Mike would win a one sided decision over rugged Scott LeDoux. Next up for Weaver was a shot at World Boxing Association titleholder Big John Tate. Many experts were saying Tate was the future of the heavyweight division. John had destroyed Bernardo Mercado, Duane Bobick and Kallie Knoetze to build a 22-0 record. He then won a convincing decision over Gerrie Coetzee to win the World Boxing Association heavyweight title vacated by Muhammad Ali. Now there was talk of Ali coming back to fight Tate. There was talk of a unification fight between Tate and Larry Holmes. The future looked very bright indeed for John Tate. The Weaver bout would just be a chance for John to showcase his talents in the friendly confines of Knoxville, Tennessee.

The bout itself pretty much went according to plan. At 6'4' and 232 pounds, Tate was a very smooth boxer for a big man. Weaver seemed somewhat lethargic in the early going, and Tate built up a substantial lead. It wasn't until around the twelfth round that Weaver stirred himself and began to open up. At one point he rocked Tate down to his toes, but John hung in there. You could see Tate was fading, but it still looked like he would be able to stall until the final bell and get the much deserved decision. The clock was ticking in round fifteen and with around a minute left in the fight, Weaver had Tate on the ropes. Mike then landed a shot to Tate's head that landed with such force that John was out before he hit the canvas. As Tate lay in a motionless heap, Mike Weaver was crowned a world champion. Poor Tate was never the same after this fight. He would be knocked out by Trevor Berbick in his next fight and then fade from contender status.

Weaver's first defense would be in South Africa against native son Gerrie Coetzee. The experts gave the hard punching Coetzee a good chance of bringing the crown to South Africa. The bout itself was an action packed contest. Each fighter landed their share of heavy punches. Weaver was landing well with powerful left hooks to the body. These seemed to be breaking Coetzee down. Weaver was slightly ahead on points when he halted Coetzee in round thirteen of a real slugfest.

Weaver's next defense would be against unbeaten (20-0) James "Quick" Tillis. It was a dreary fifteen round affair that saw Tillis take few chances. Weaver retained his title with a convincing decision. Next for Mike, there would be undefeated (24-0-1) Michael Dokes at Caesar's Palace in Las Vegas. The bout had hardly started, when Dokes stunned Weaver and sent him to the ropes. Dokes was quickly on Weaver trying to follow up. Weaver was trying to defend himself when referee Joey Curtis jumped in and stopped the fight! Only one minute and three seconds had elapsed and now Mike Weaver was an ex-champion. It was a very controversial ending, and a rematch was scheduled. The second meeting took place five months later. It was a solid action fight with both boxers dishing out their fair share of punishment. I felt Weaver came on down the stretch to do enough to regain his title. His bodywork was excellent as he gave Dokes quite a rib roasting. Two judges scored the fight a draw. The other judge had Dokes four points ahead. Dokes retained his title with a draw. To this day I still feel Mike Weaver won that fight.

Weaver would solidify his status as a top contender again stopping Stan Ward in their rubber match. Then almost two years after his draw with Dokes, Weaver was set to meet WBC champion Pinklon Thomas. This was a good scrap while it lasted. Thomas had a great jab, but at times Weaver was out jabbing him. Mike was also landing some heavy body shots. Although Weaver had suffered a brief knockdown in the first round, he had battled back and the bout was almost dead even after seven rounds. In the eighth round Weaver's chin betrayed him as Thomas knocked him out to retain his title.

From this point on, the career of Mike Weaver became a roller coaster. He scored a second round kayo over highly regarded Carl "The Truth" Williams. Then in turn, he was taken out in one round by James

"Bonecrusher" Smith. Next Mike would lose a split decision to Donovan "Razor" Ruddock. Fifteen months later Weaver would return to South Africa and upset Johnny DuPlooy in seven rounds. Five months later Weaver would return to South Africa again, but this time DuPlooy took him out in the second.

In April of 1990 Mike would lose a lopsided decision in a rematch with "Bonecrusher" Smith. Over a year later, he was belted out in six rounds by an up and coming Lennox Lewis. The loss to Lewis pretty much finished Weaver as a serious contender. In 1993 he was on the big fight card in China and won a hard fought ten round decision over Bert Cooper. Mike won his next five fights over mediocre competition. In 1998 weighing in at 244 pounds, he was halted by Melvin Foster in nine rounds.

Over two years later in his last hurrah, Weaver got his long awaited rematch with Larry Holmes. This time Larry was the boss as he stopped Weaver in round six. It was Mike's last fight. Weaver retired after sixty pro fights with a record of 41-18-1. He scored 28 knockouts and was stopped 12 times. Sometimes records are deceiving. From Weaver's 1974 loss to Duane Bobick up to his 1985 title fight with Pinklon Thomas, Mike had a 21-4-1 record. Mike met seven world champions and five others who fought for the titles.

CHUCK WEPNER

During his formidable professional career heavyweight boxer Chuck Wepner was known as the "Bayonne Bleeder". Hundreds of stitches had adorned his rugged face throughout his career. After his fighting days were over, Chuck has become known to his legion of fans as the "Real Life Rocky", the inspiration for Sylvester Stallone's film character Rocky Balboa.

Wepner was born on February 26, 1939, in New York. He was the son of a heavyweight boxer, and as an amateur, he won the 1964 New York Golden Gloves Novice heavyweight title. He then turned professional. In his first two years in the paid ranks, he went 4-1-2 losing only to tough Bob Stallings. On January 7, 1966, Chuck met highly regarded prospect Buster Mathis at Madison Square Garden. Wepner was halted in the third round. In 1967 Wepner would win the New Jersey State heavyweight title stopping Don McAteer in the seventh.

Chuck went undefeated in 1968 winning six fights. He beat Eddie Vick and upset highly regarded Forest Ward. In 1969 Wepner defeated Roberto Davila but then lost to future heavyweight title challenger Joe "King" Roman. On August 18th he met 1968 Olympic Gold Medalist George Foreman at the Garden. Chuck was stopped in the third round. Wepner finished the year by outscoring veteran Pedro Agosto. Chuck opened 1970 by defeating former world title challenger Manuel Ramos. On June 29th Chuck would meet former world champion Sonny Liston. Sonny cut the game Wepner to ribbons, and the bout was ended after the ninth round. Chuck then traveled to London to meet another future world title challenger named Joe Bugner. A cut forced Wepner to exit in round three.

As 1971 rolled in, Wepner was again badly cut, forcing a stoppage against Jerry Judge. Chuck would then lose his New Jersey title to smooth boxing Randy Neumann. The two would meet again in 1972, and Wepner pulled out the decision to regain the New Jersey crown. This would be the beginning of an eight bout win streak that would lead Chuck to a crack at the world title. On June 23, 1973, Wepner pulled off a major upset in Atlantic City winning a controversial twelve round decision over former World Boxing Association heavyweight champion Ernie Terrell. Chuck was now rated among the top ten heavyweights in the world. He solidified his ranking in 1974 by defeating Randy Neumann in their rubber match and stopping Terry Hinke.

The stage was now set. On March 24, 1975, Wepner would meet world champion Muhammad Ali at the Richfield Coliseum outside on the outskirts of Cleveland, Ohio. Ali had shocked the world in October of 1974 by regaining the heavyweight title defeating George Foreman. He was looking for an easy defense of that title. Although Wepner was ranked, few, if any, gave him a real chance at defeating Ali. What transpired that day made Chuck Wepner a cult hero. Ali won and retained his crown, but it was hardly the walk in the park he expected. Wepner hadn't read the Ali script. In fact Chuck became the script for Rocky. Despite scoring a debatable knockdown over Ali in the ninth round, Chuck was battered throughout the contest. Ali punished Wepner, but try as he might, he couldn't put Chuck away. Finally the dead game Wepner fell in the fifteenth and final round. It was more from exhaustion then Ali's punches, a true testimony to Chuck's grit and courage.

After the Ali fight, the career of Wepner slowly wound down. He was cut and stopped by undefeated prospect Duane Bobick in 1976. In 1977 he dropped a decision to Mike Schutte. He was then halted in the tenth round by Horst Geisler. Chuck won two fights in 1978, but then lost a decision to yet another future title challenger, Scott Frank. That would be Wepner's last fight.

Chuck retired with a record of 35-14-2. During his career he met four world champions and five others that challenged for the crown.

CLEVELAND "BIG CAT" WILLIAMS

When Cleveland "Big Cat" Williams passed away a few years back, it ended the final chapter of a story about three gifted heavyweights from the 50's and 60's. Williams joined Eddie Machen and Zora Folley to form a trio of hard luck boxers who met tragic deaths after a career of frustration. Machen lost a decision to Ernie Terrell in a 1965 W.B.A. title bout. Later Eddie suffered some mental problems and eventually committed suicide. Folley who was stopped in seven by Muhammad Ali in 1967 died of injuries suffered in a poolside accident. Machen and Folley passed on several years ago. Williams lived to be 66 before being struck down by a moving vehicle. All three would finally receive their title shots long after their prime. One wonders how they would have made out if they got their chance five years earlier against Floyd

Patterson. To Floyd's credit, he did win a twelve round decision over Machen in 1964, two years after he lost his crown to Sonny Liston.

Williams began his career in 1951 and won his first 27 fights, 23 by knockout. In 1954, he suffered a knockout loss to Bob Satterfield. Cleveland did not box in 1955, because he was in the Army. When he resumed his career, he ran off 12 straight wins leading him to a match with the feared Sonny Liston. The two traded bombs until Sonny put over the sleeper in round two. Eleven months later they met again in another war with Sonny winning in round three.

In Cleveland's next 22 fights, he went 20-1-1 with 13 kayos. He lost a decision to Terrell, and he drew with Machen. He scored victories over Terrell, Wayne Bethea, Alex Miteff, Billy Daniels, and Tod Herring. This led to a title bout with Muhammad Ali in November of 1966. In 1965, Williams was badly injured when he was shot by a patrolman during a traffic stop argument. The bullet entered his stomach doing severe damage. That he was even able to fight again, is a testimony to his will and courage. The Williams that entered the ring against Ali was just a shell of his former self. In what many feel was Ali's best career performance, the champion dominated his aging rival. The bout was mercifully stopped in the third round. Cleveland would never again be a major factor in the division. He lost to Bob Cleroux and Mac Foster and served as an opponent for upcoming fighters looking for a name on their record.

I had the opportunity to see Williams box a decent heavy weight named Ted Gullick at the old Cleveland Arena. Gullick would meet George Foreman, Ernie Shavers, and Duane Bobick during his career, but he was no match for Williams this night. Using a ramrod jab and a solid body attack, Cleveland out boxed his upstart foe to win a ten rounder. The consummate professional at work, that is how I'll remember Cleveland Williams.

TIM WITHERSPOON

In my opinion one of the most under rated heavyweights over the last twenty years has been "Terrible" Tim Witherspoon. He was a two time world champion and a solid contender for close to two decades. This man DESERVES some recognition.

Tim, a native of the great fight city of Philadelphia, turned pro in 1979. He won his first fifteen fights beating the likes of Marvin Stinson, Alonzo Ratliff and Renaldo Snipes. This led to a 1983 title shot against the respected Larry Holmes. Larry walked away with a highly controversial decision win. Despite the loss, the "Terrible" one had arrived.

Tim rebounded outscoring Jumbo Cummings and blasting out James "Quick" Tillis in one for the NABF title. In 1984 Witherspoon was matched with the talented Greg Page for the vacant WBC title. On this night Tim would outscore Page to win his first title. In his first defense, Tim was out jabbed and out boxed by the speedy Pinklon Thomas. "Pinky" put on a class performance that night.

Witherspoon came back in 1985 to halt tough Mark Wills and score a highlight reel KO over James Broad. Tim then outpointed James "Bonecrusher" Smith. This led to a shot at the WBA title against fast handed Tony Tubbs. In 1986 Tim won the heavyweight title for a second time with a decision over Tubbs. He then defended it with a sensational come from behind KO of England's heralded Frank Bruno. In Tim's next defense, the walls came tumbling down. He met "Bonecrusher" again. This was a man he had defeated handily the first time around. This time Tim was caught cold and dropped three times in the first round. His title was gone. He would never again get a well-deserved chance to reclaim it.

In 1987 he halted Mark Wills again, this time in the first round. He then outscored prospect Mike Williams. In 1989 Tim scored a stunning one round KO over Anders Eklund who resembled a blond tree being felled. Witherspoon was back in business. In 1990 he halted dangerous Jeff Sims. Then he outscored Jose Ribalta and later defeated the flashy Carl

"The Truth" Williams for the USBA title. In 1991 he took out Art Tucker in three. To his credit, Tim ducked no one.

In 1992 Witherspoon beat rugged James Pritchard. Tim was then upset by the spoiler Everett "Big Foot" Martin. In 1996 he outscored Alfred Cole and bombed out Jorge Luis Gonzalez. Next Tim would lose a war to, tough as nails, Ray Mercer. From this point Tim's career was up and down. He took out Levi Billips in one. He dropped verdicts to Larry Donald, Jimmy Thunder and Andrew Golota. In 1999 he was halted by Brian Nielsen and Greg Page. His career appeared to be over.

Tim made one last charge in 2000. He drew with Mike Sedillo. He then halted David Bostice in one. He upset Elieser Castillo but dropped a points call to Monte Barrett. Tim then gave us one last highlight clip KO dropping Darroll Wilson. In 2002 the aging Witherspoon was savaged in five rounds by Lou Savarese. In 2003 Tim dropped a decision to Brian Nix and called it quits.

Witherspoon ended his career with a 55-13-1 ledger against the best heavyweights of his era. He knocked out 38 foes, several in spectacular fashion. He was only halted four times. He was tough, strong, powerful and durable. Sometimes his lack of training and dedication may have held him back. Nevertheless in my humble opinion, a well-conditioned and prime Witherspoon would have been a handful for a peak "Iron" Mike Tyson. Too bad that fight never happened.

JAMES J. WOODY

Although he ended his career losing almost as many bouts as he won, one-time 1960's heavyweight James J. Woody was considered a fine prospect when his career started.

He was from the Bronx who had his first professional fight in 1964. He reeled off ten straight wins against better than average competition. He twice defeated Lou Hicks and also the giant James J. Beattie a couple of times. He also won a duet from Everett Copeland and outscored Tony Doyle.

He suffered his first loss to the crafty Johnny Persol in 1966. That began years of winning a few and losing a few for Woody. At times he was good enough to beat decent fighters like Dante Cane, Roger Russell and Charlie "Emperor" Harris. At other times he was overmatched at that stage in his career against contenders Manuel Ramos, Brian London and Big Buster Mathis losing to all three.

On April 17, 1970, he faced the feared Olympian George Foreman. The undefeated future two time world champion was impressive bombing out Woody in the third round.

In his next bout James faced the highly regarded Oscar Bonavena and was stopped in five. Later that year, Bonavena would meet the returning Muhammad Ali in their classic fifteen round encounter.

James would bounce back into the win column with a pair of decision victories over the hexed Tony Doyle. Those would be his last victories.

In 1971 James would prove he was no chump as he went the distance in rugged bouts with top contenders Jose Luis Garcia, Ken Norton and in 1972 to Henry Clark. Although he lost all three, they were all competitive, especially the Norton fight. He met Norton again in 1972, and Kenny halted James in eight. In 1973 James was toppled in two rounds by the resurging Jerry Quarry. In 1974 James was halted by Bob Stallings. He returned two years later on the Ali-Norton III undercard at Yankee Stadium in his hometown of the Bronx. There he was taken out in three rounds by up and coming Bernardo Mercado.

JIMMY YOUNG

The glorious 1970's was the era of Ali and Frazier, of Foreman, Norton and later Holmes, and of bangers like Ron Lyle, Jerry Quarry and Earnie Shavers. Then there was a smooth boxing, counter-punching master named Jimmy Young. This wily heavyweight from Philadelphia would lose a highly controversial verdict to Ali in a title fight. He would then upset George Foreman but lose another heartbreaking decision to Ken Norton for the World Boxing

Council title. Jimmy Young was so close and yet so far. He had two shots at the championship and came out on the short end of two debatable decisions. Then, just like that, he went from contender to trial horse to also run.

In his prime, as I would like to remember Jimmy Young, he was one heck of a fighter. Jimmy twice outscored the feared Ron Lyle. He was stopped by Earnie Shavers (no shame there), but he also drew with Shavers. Everyone knows that his claim to fame was gutting out a painfully terrible seventh round and then coming back to outlast and out punch an exhausted George Foreman in a major upset. Big George would not fight again for ten years!

Before Jimmy beat Foreman he had met an aging Muhammad Ali for the world's title. It was obvious that training was not a top priority for Muhammad. He must have taken Jimmy very lightly. The fight turned out to be a real stinker that went to the scorecards after fifteen rounds. Ali got the verdict and retained his crown. Many felt Jimmy did enough to win. I disagree with that. It was a close but utterly boring tussle. Young had his moments but his ducking through the ropes to avoid punishment did not endear him to the fans or the judges.

When Jimmy rebounded from the Ali setback and defeated Foreman, it led to a match with #1 contender Ken Norton. Ali had lost his title to Olympian Leon Spinks. The W.B.C. wanted Leon to defend against the deserving Norton. Leon opted for a lucrative return against Ali. The W.B.C. then stripped Leon and matched Norton with Young. Although I thought Jimmy lost to Ali or should I say he didn't do enough to take the title, I thought he earned the nod against Norton in a hard fought competitive battle. Kenny won the decision and the recognition of the W.B.C. as titleholder. Jimmy then lost two decisions to Ossie Ocasio, and that began his fade into boxing oblivion.

Jimmy was not an exciting fighter, but he was well schooled. He was a real master of his craft. He had a stinging jab. He was a slick defensive boxer who was very good at making his opponent miss and then counter. He had a good right hand that had some pop to it. He was also a decent body puncher who was not afraid to mix it up on the inside. He was not overly great at one thing but was very adept at doing a lot of things.

He reminded me a lot of the great light heavyweight champion Harold Johnson, an outstanding fighter who is often overlooked because of his conservative style. I guess the best way to describe Harold and Jimmy is that they were consummate professionals.

PART TWO

ALI - FRAZIER I; THE GREATEST SHOW ON EARTH

There are certain dates that will stick with you as long as you live, your birthday, the birthdays of family members, anniversaries, the day that you got your divorce (s), etc…happy and important days that mark milestones in your life.

One such date I'll always remember is March 8, 1971. The "Battle of the Century", it was so aptly named. Two undefeated boxers who each had a legitimate claim to being the heavyweight champion of the world would collide. When Muhammad Ali first won the title in 1964, his name was Cassius Clay. He would shortly thereafter change his name and then proceed to change the face of boxing. He dominated the scene until 1967 when he refused induction into the United States military due to his religious beliefs. The infamous World Boxing Association Eight Man Elimination Tourney that was won by Jimmy Ellis then came. The powerful New York State Athletic Commission would recognize the winner of a matchup between unbeaten boxers Joe Frazier and Buster Mathis, a bout in which Joe won. In 1970 Frazier stopped Ellis to claim the universal title. Later that year Muhammad Ali returned to the ring wars and halted the highly ranked contenders Jerry Quarry and Oscar Bonavena. The stage was now set. Ali and Frazier would clash for the undisputed title.

The first Ali – Frazier bout was the epic that all others are compared to, even today. There is no reason in this article to describe the bout itself. Reams of print have appeared documenting the action that took place in the ring that magical night. What I would like to share is the impact that fight had on me and probably millions of others. I have never before or since March 8, 1971, felt the same way about a prize fight. Yes there were a few that stirred my anticipation to a high degree like Duran-Dejesus III, Leonard-Duran I, Leonard-Hearns I, Pryor-Arguello I, Hagler-Hearns and Leonard-Hagler. Still to this day Ali – Frazier I tops them all.

Was the first Ali – Frazier bout the best action fight of all time? I would have to say no but for sheer anticipation, drama and excitement this fight was the whole package. You had movie star Burt Lancaster as a commentator and Frank Sinatra as a photographer. Each boxer would receive $ 2.5 million for their nights work. That was an unheard sum of money for one fight in 1971.

I have never been so wound up with anticipation for a boxing match in my life. I was a few months shy of my seventeenth birthday and had been a boxing fan from the time I was ten. I had closely followed all the events leading up to this day in boxing history. I could not wait.

On fight night I was at a party, and we gathered around the radio listening to the round by round summary. We were pretty much split on the outcome of the fight but almost all of us were rooting for "Smokin' Joe". From the round by round reports we could sense that this was a bout with shifting momentums. The ever proud Ali realized that Joe had come to fight this evening. Maybe Ali took Frazier too lightly. Maybe Muhammad rushed too soon to get back in the ring after his lengthy layoff. Maybe, just maybe the Joe Frazier of March 8, 1971, was one of the greatest heavyweights of all time. I've never seen a boxer who laid it all out for one fight like Joe did that night. You've heard it said that a boxer would rather die than be defeated. On this night Joe would have died a hundred deaths before giving in to Ali.

Round after round went by, and as we listened to the radio reports, in the eleventh Frazier rocked Ali, and we as a collective group cheered, even the ones who had bet on Ali to win. As the bout moved into the "championship" rounds, we were all on the edge of our seats. Then it happened. It was announced on the radio that Joe had decked Ali in the fifteenth round, more cheering and now the wait. Finally it was time to render the decision. The winner and still heavyweight champion of the world…Joe Frazier! Oh what a night. So many years later I can still remember it like it was yesterday.

Joe Frazier has passed on and Ali, my friends and I are in the twilight of our lives. Still when I think of that night, it takes me back to my youth and to the ultimate excitement that probably the greatest single sporting event of all time brought me. Thanks Joe and Muhammad.

WHAT IF? LISTON -VS- JOHANSSON IN 1961

Champion Ingemar Johansson vs Sonny Liston was a fight that very well could have happened. After Ingo shocked Floyd Patterson to win the title in 1959, he was the "man." At this time Sonny was just beginning to establish himself as a heavyweight to be reckoned with. By the time Floyd and Ingo met again in June of 1960, Sonny had defeated Nino Valdez and Cleveland Williams twice. One month after Patterson - Johansson II, Sonny stopped the clever Zora Folley. Then two months later he outscored the classy Eddie Machen. There was little doubt that Sonny Liston would have to be dealt with.

Think about this: What if Ingemar would have won his 1960 bout with Patterson? There would have been no need for a 1961 rubber match with Floyd. Enter Sonny. He would have been the most logical contender. So how would a match between Johansson and Liston pan out in June of 1961?

ROUND 1: They both come out jabbing. Ingemar is pawing with his jab using it as a range finder for his "Thunder of Thor" right hand. Sonny is putting more behind his jab, and they are snapping Johansson's head back. They are finally on the inside, and Ingo is holding his own.

After the referee breaks them, the two again are in a jabbing contest. Finally, Johansson lets the right hand fly over Sonny's extended jab, and it connects. It actually sends Sonny back a step. Ingo moves in, but he is met by a solid jab and a thudding right to the body. They wrestle around on the inside at the bell.

Liston's jab won a close round for him, but Ingemar landed the first damaging punch.

ROUND 2: Sonny is really pumping the jab and has Johansson on the defensive. Ingemar is trying to get under the jab, but on the inside Sonny is landing heavy, looping body shots that hurt. Ingo is game, and he is trying to launch his vaunted right hand. Sonny's jab is keeping Ingemar of balance and unable to get the full power behind the right. Ingo's nose is bleeding, and he has several large red welts on his midsection.

Liston controlled the round and is now up two rounds to none.

ROUND 3: Sonny is sticking to his game plan, and the jab is doing a lot of damage. Ingemar keeps trying, but he is telegraphing the right hand, and Sonny is paying attention. Finally Ingo gets one in, and Sonny again stumbles back a few steps. The crowd is on their feet. As Johansson moves in, Sonny lands a monster left hook to Ingo's jaw that sends him to his knees. The courageous Johansson is up at eight, but Sonny shuffles right after him. Ingemar lets a desperate right fly, and it catches Sonny on the top of his head and stops Sonny's attack for the moment. Liston shoots in a few jabs as the round comes to a close.

With the knockdown Sonny gets a 10-8 round.

ROUND 4: Ingemar comes out winging but does not land any effective shots. Sonny remains calm and starts planting that jab again. Ingo is starting to become weary, and Liston starts doing more work on the inside. Johansson tries to tie Sonny up, but Liston will have none of it. Sonny works Ingo to the ropes, and he is just raking him with body blows. Finally a tremendous uppercut to the jaw sends Ingo sprawling to the canvas. Johansson shows true grit as he is up at nine. The referee hesitates a moment and then waves the two fighters together. Liston walks back in and is literally throwing bombs. Ingo is trying to survive but each shot lands with a telling effect. A left hook slams into Johansson's jaw, and he sags to the canvas just as the referee has grabbed Liston from behind to hold him back.

It's over. The bout has been stopped at the 1:58 second mark of round four. The winner and new champion of the world, Sonny Liston!

Ingemar is helped up by his corner men and led back to his corner. He appears to be OK. A good sportsman, Sonny comes over to check on Ingo, and they shake hands. As Sonny is being interviewed he praises Johansson's courage. He also said that Ingemar was the hardest puncher he ever met including Cleveland Williams. Sonny even admitted that he was stunned a few times.

Johansson when interviewed seemed disappointed in losing his title. He said he could not believe Sonny absorbed his best shots and kept coming. He also said that Liston hurts you every time he lands a punch no matter where it lands. He predicted a long reign for Sonny and expressed no interest in a rematch.

WHEN LEOTIS MADE THEM NOTICE

In December of 1969 Charles "Sonny" Liston the former heavyweight champion of the world was in the midst of a remarkable comeback. Following his disastrous kayo losses to Cassius Clay (Muhammad Ali), Sonny was written off by the experts. While Ali dominated the heavyweight scene, Sonny took some time off. When Sonny did embark on a comeback, he went to Europe and reeled off a series of wins against some non-threatening pugilists. He returned to the U.S. with little fanfare and continued his low key comeback with victories over the likes of Roger Rischter, Amos Lincoln, Billy Joiner etc…

While Sonny's comeback moved at a snail's pace, the heavyweight picture was changing dramatically. When Ali refused induction into the

Armed Forces, he was stripped of his title and forced into idleness. It seemed very likely that Ali would never box again. A series of elimination bouts produced two championship claimants, Jimmy Ellis and Joe Frazier. With Ali out of the way, Sonny felt confident that he could take either Ellis or Frazier. It was now time for Sonny to make his move.

Sonny's first serious test on his comeback campaign would come against young Henry Clark. At first some experts thought Sonny made a mistake in choosing Clark. In his previous comeback bouts, Sonny still seemed to carry his vaunted power, but he also looked slow and ponderous. Clark was not a big puncher, but he was a boxer and a mover in the Ali style, a style that had proven in the past to trouble Sonny. The actual fight was comparable to a man against a boy. Only Clark's gameness made it competitive. The referee finally raised Sonny's hand in round seven. Liston was now right back in the thick of the heavyweight picture. Sonny said he wanted to fight Jerry Quarry and then either Ellis or Frazier.

The next step for Sonny would be against veteran contender Leotis Martin. Martin had lost to Ellis in the first round of the now infamous World Boxing Association's elimination tournament, and he also lost to Henry Clark. He seemed like a "safe" opponent. A win for Sonny here may get him a shot at the winner of the Ellis-Frazier unification bout that was scheduled for February of 1970. The bout started slowly with Liston forcing the action behind his long punishing left jab. At times Martin was able to jab with him, but Sonny was in control. In round four Sonny finally connected with a long sweeping left hook that floored Martin by the ropes. Leotis survived the round and actually began picking up the pace in round five. After six rounds Sonny was well out in front, but Martin was very much alive and there were six rounds to go. In the seventh Sonny seemed to age in front of everyone's eyes. Martin was beginning to out jab Sonny while also landing effective counter shots. In the eighth round Liston became unglued. Martin bloodied and cut Liston's nose, and the blood poured into Sonny's mouth impairing his breathing. In round nine Liston seemed to just be trying to box his way to the final bell in hopes that his early lead would get him the decision. Martin had other plans. Leotis was now punishing Liston with wicked jabs to his gory face. Sonny's jab was more of a flicking jab. As Liston pawed out with a series of jabs, Martin timed the last one perfectly and came over the top with a crunching overhand right. The punch literally froze Sonny in his tracks. Swiftly Leotis connected with a powerful left hook to the chin and another right as Sonny fell face first to the canvas, OUT COLD! In a matter of seconds the aura and myth of Sonny Liston was shattered. As announcer Howard Cosell called it a "crushing and compelling knockout."

WHAT IF? RON LYLE VERSUS KEN NORTON

It should have happened. It could have happened. Ken Norton and Ron Lyle, both are two of the best heavyweights of the "Glorious 70's" era of boxing, and they could have created quite a stir if they would have met. By 1973 Ron Lyle was an upcoming, undefeated prospect, while Norton was already a contender due to his win over clever Henry Clark. In February of 1973 Lyle made his Madison Square Garden debut and was taken to school by veteran tough guy Jerry Quarry. One month later Norton shocked the world when he broke Muhammad Ali's jaw and scored a well-deserved upset decision.

Norton was now a star and a close decision loss to Ali in a rematch established Kenny as a major player. The two bouts with Ali garnered Norton a title shot against George Foreman. This fight was a disaster for Kenny as he was halted in the second round. In the meantime Lyle would fight his way back into contention.

Only the slick Jimmy Young would sidetrack Ron. In 1975 Lyle would meet new champion Muhammad Ali for the title. Ron did well in a slow, strategic fight, but in the eleventh Ali hurt Lyle. The champ opened up, and the referee stopped the contest. In 1976 Norton would get his rubber match with Ali with the title on the line at Yankee Stadium. Ali got the verdict, but I, along with many others, thought Norton should have won the crown that night.

In 1977 Norton would be awarded the World Boxing Council version of the title with a points win over Jimmy Young. I myself thought the hard luck Young won a close fight. In 1978 Norton would lose the crown in a classic battle to Larry Holmes. Kenny was then crushed in one round by Earnie Shavers. He barely survived to salvage a draw against rough and tumble Scott LeDoux. He did edge Randy "Tex" Cobb but then came his scary one round loss to Gerry Cooney.

Ron Lyle would never get another shot at the title. After he lost to Ali, he came back to out slug Earnie Shavers in a war. Then Ron would lose in one of the greatest heavyweight fights in history when George Foreman got off the canvas to stop Lyle. Jimmy Young would again out smart Lyle, and although Ron remained a contender, he was never again a front runner.

Why did this fight not take place? Good question. One reason I believe is that Norton rose to the top quicker and made a name for himself with his bone breaking win over Ali. From that point on, he had star power, and he could be a little more selective with his opponents. I don't feel that Ken feared Lyle, but I think he realized he did not have Jake LaMotta's jaw. Ron Lyle could punch. Why take a chance against a guy like that when Ken always seemed to be in the thick of the heavyweight picture. Lyle needed Norton more than Ken needed him.

Who would have won? Lyle was a better boxer than given credit for. He could punch, and he had a pretty good chin. Norton was a sharp hitter, but he was not a devastating puncher. I just believe Ron could have taken Ken's shots. I don't believe Norton would have held up under Lyle's attack. My pick would have been Lyle by a knockout.

One other thing, after researching this article, I came to remember just how good a fighter Jimmy Young was.

WHAT IF? JIMMY ELLIS VERSUS BOB FOSTER IN 1969

In April of 1967, Jimmy Ellis pounded out a fifteen round decision over Jerry Quarry to win the vacant W.B.A. heavyweight championship. In March of 1968, Joe Frazier halted Buster Mathis to win heavyweight title recognition in New York State. Two months later Bob Foster knocked out the great Dick Tiger to capture the light heavyweight crown. Foster felt the big money was in the heavyweight division, and he began to challenge the champions. Frazier actively defended his title turning back Manuel Ramos, Jerry Quarry, Oscar Bonevena, and Dave Zyglewicz. Ellis, on the other hand, made only one defense, a disputed verdict over ex-champion Floyd Patterson. Proposed matches for Jimmy against Henry Cooper, Gregorio Peralta and Robert Cleroux never materialized. By the time Ellis met Frazier in February of 1970 to unify the crown, the ring rust had settled in. After Frazier destroyed Ellis, he would go on to meet Foster later on that year with disastrous results for Bob.

What if during his period of idleness before the Frazier debate had Ellis entertained Foster's challenge? Foster, as we would find out, could not handle Frazier's power, strength and aggression. How would he have fared against a master boxer like Ellis? It may have gone something like this.

The 198 pound Ellis strides out to meet the 181-pound Foster to begin round one. Quickly they began to trade jabs. Jimmy is quicker, but Foster is harder and more accurate. By the middle of the round it is apparent that this is becoming a chess match. Then out of nowhere Ellis connects with a whistling overhand right, and Foster is shaken. Bob stumbles back against the ropes, and Ellis is right on him. Jimmy just misses with another right and then connects with a hard left hook to the head, and Bob's in serious trouble. Ellis is winging at Foster who can't seem to get away from the ropes. Then in a wild exchange Foster hurts Ellis with a short left hook. Momentarily stunned, Ellis takes a few steps back, and now Foster is jabbing his way off the ropes. Ellis comes in and connects with another overhand right, but this one lands high on Foster's head. In another heated exchange they both land left hooks, but Foster's does more damage. Ellis now has a small cut on his right eyelid as the bell sounds ending the round.

Angelo Dundee the manager-trainer of Ellis is giving Jimmy a tongue lashing in the corner. Ellis comes out fast for round two and takes a couple of hard jabs. In return he lands a hard left hook to the body that makes Bob wince. Foster's trying to slow down the pace but Ellis, his ears still ringing from Dundee's tirade, continues to press. Foster is landing more punches, but Jimmy's body punches are bothering Bob. As Ellis moves in, Foster catches him with a jab, and then he slams in a short chopping right flush on the jaw, and Ellis sinks to one knee. Jimmy takes an eight count shaking his head as he's trying to clear the cobwebs. As Foster comes in, Jimmy clinches. On the inside Ellis is much stronger, and he lands some effective punches to Bob's lean rib cage. Jimmy appears to be all right now, but he's staying close to smother Fosters punches.

Dundee is livid in the corner between rounds while Foster has a smug look. He knows he can hurt Ellis now. Ellis is still trying to stay close in round three. Bob is using his jab to good effect, and Jimmy's cut has been re-opened. Bob is trying to shorten up his left hook hoping that will discourage Ellis from coming inside. Jimmy's making the fight, but Foster's landing the more effective blows. As Bob dips down to throw a short left hook, Ellis lets go of a vicious overhand right that catches Foster flush on the jaw, and Bob goes down flat on his back. He begins to get up at "6" and just barely beats the count. The referee asks Bob if he's all right. Foster says yes, but his eyes are unfocused. The referee lets it continue, and Ellis is on him in a flash. Another overhand right lands, but it's a little off target. Still it wobbled Bob who makes a feeble attempt to jab. Ellis slips inside and lands a tremendous left hook to Foster's chin, and Bob crumbles to the canvas. There will be no count as Foster's cornermen comes to his aid.

At 175 pounds Bob Foster was possibly the best light heavyweight of all time. He just did not have the strength to battle the big boys. Doug

Jones, Zora Folley and Ernie Terrell all handled Bob easily in his pre-championship days.

Jimmy Ellis earned his title by beating Leotis Martin, Oscar Bonevena and Jerry Quarry. No easy task. Ellis was a deceptively hard puncher. He had the granite chinned Bonevena down twice. Also he nearly had Leotis Martin out in the first round of their fight.

ALI AND THE ACORN

It was to be the last time the incomparable Muhammad Ali would ever successfully defend the heavyweight championship. It would be held in boxing's most famous arena, Madison Square Garden. It would also feature Ohio's most popular heavyweight of the last quarter century, Earnie Shavers. The "Acorn", as Ali had dubbed Shavers, would be a prohibitive underdog. He was accorded a puncher's chance at best against the aging but still crafty king of the heavyweights. What transpired the night of September 29, 1977, established Earnie as a legitimate contender and forecasted the soon to be demise of "The Greatest".

The playful Ali continually mocked Earnie during the pre-fight introductions by rubbing the top of the "Acorn's" head. In this fight the scorecards would be made public as the battle was being contested. Everyone would know the score as the fight was progressing, an idea that has gladly never caught on. The relaxed and confident Ali easily out boxed Earnie in round one and was doing the same in round two. Then out of nowhere a crackling Shavers right hand stunned Ali and sent him wobbling backwards. Hurt and glassy eyed Ali waved Earnie in. Again Shavers landed with dynamite force staggering Ali. Only Muhammad's tremendous heart, chin and cunning enabled him to survive the round. Action slowed in the middle rounds as Ali mugged to the crowd, and several times he would lie on the ropes and try to lure Earnie in. Shavers refused to become a victim of the "Rope-A-Dope", and the crowd booed wanting more action. They got it as the bout progressed past the seventh round. On numerous occasions Earnie rocked the champion back on his heels with explosive right hand bombs. When Ali kept his distance, he dominated with sharp jabs and straight rights.

Going into the late rounds Ali had the lead, but in rounds twelve, thirteen and fourteen Earnie fought probably the best three rounds of his career. Several times he stunned a tired but dead game Ali. Many thought Earnie would tire since he had never fought past ten rounds, but it was Ali who appeared to be wilting.

The fifteenth round saw two desperate warriors engaging in a thrilling toe-to-toe slugfest. Ali seemed revived, and Earnie was letting it all hang out in a last ditch effort to win the crown. Earnie edged Ali during the first two minutes of the round, and then he finally tired. Ali came on and hurt Earnie for the first time in the bout. Showing a remarkable will to survive, Shavers refused to fall, although he was beaten around the ring. At last the final bell sounded saving Earnie and putting his fate in the scorecards.

The final scoring: 9-6, 9-6 and 9-5-1 for the winner and still champion, Muhammad Ali. The crowd lustily booed the verdict. Whether you agreed or disagreed with the decision, one thing was certainly unanimous among the crowd, Earnie Shavers had arrived.

WHAT IF? FOREMAN -VS- QUARRY IN 1973

Super Fights...it is a very over used term these days. Some of the PPV "Super Fights" of today would have been nice Saturday afternoon feature bouts on ABC's Wide World of Sports in my day.

There were several bouts from the late 1960's to the early 1980's I wish would have been made. These are bouts that actually had been rumored in the making or someone's wishful thinking. If some of these bouts had taken place, it could have altered the history of boxing forever.

In January of 1973 big George Foreman disrupted the plans of an Ali - Frazier rematch. George gave Joe as one sided a whipping as you'll ever see. One month later a "washed up" Jerry Quarry derailed the Ron

Lyle express to the championship. Then in March Ken Norton broke the hearts of Ali fans while cracking the jaw of the "Greatest".

Just like that, in a span of three months the whole top tier of the heavyweight ranks had been seriously shuffled. Ali and Frazier were no longer the kings of the hill. There were a couple of new kids on the block named George and Kenny. Also a grizzled old veteran had returned to town.

To me the one fight that should have been made from this abrupt restructuring of the big boys was Jerry Quarry -vs- George Foreman. The ever popular Irishman had lost to Frazier in 1969 and to Ali in 1970 and 1972. Still Jerry always found a way to stay in the thick of the heavyweight picture. The win over the previously unbeaten Lyle made Jerry a major player again.

This bout would have sold out Madison Square Garden in no time at all. On paper it looked like it would have been a relatively safe defense for George. Add to the fact that George was much bigger and stronger then Jerry. It is hard to believe that this fight was not made. Quarry pleaded for a shot at George, and he gave the impression that he was very confident that he could whip Foreman. It was rumored that Jerry had once handled a then young George with relative ease in a sparring session.

To the surprise of many, the Foreman camp seemed to be uninterested in a lucrative bout with Quarry. Frazier was still beat up, and Ali had to mend his jaw and then his reputation in a return with Norton. Lyle was eliminated, so Jerry seemed to be the logical choice. Instead George would meet and defeat Joe "King" Roman in his only other 1973 appearance.

Later in 1973 Ali would win a narrow decision over Norton. Quarry would close out 1973 by halting the feared Earnie Shavers in one round.

In January of 1974 Ali and Frazier would finally meet again with Ali taking the verdict. In March Foreman would turn back the challenge of Ken Norton in less than two rounds. Quarry was on the outside looking in as Foreman and Ali announced they were meeting each other later that year in Africa.

In June of 1974 Jerry would again meet Joe Frazier in an elimination bout. Although many gave Jerry a good chance to win, it was he who was brutally eliminated in five rounds. It sure would have been nice if Quarry and Foreman would have met some hot summer night at Madison Square Garden in 1973. What a fight that may have been!

HOW I REMEMBER SMOKIN' JOE FRAZIER

The sport of boxing lost a true legend with the passing of former heavyweight champion Joe Frazier. So much of my early days following boxing had to do with Joe Frazier. I was only ten years old when he won the Olympic Gold Medal in 1964. I remember how impressed I was seeing a photo of a smiling Frazier with his hands raised above his head in the sports page. This was after halting the rugged George Chuvalo in 1967. This was the same Chuvalo who went the distance with Muhammad Ali in a title fight the year before. I knew then Frazier would be a champion one day.

I remember when Ali was stripped of his title and Joe was held out of the WBA Eight Man Elimination tourney by his astute manager Yancey Durham. Joe would then beat the large but clever Buster Mathis to win title recognition in New York and Pennsylvania. When the dust settled in the eight man box off, Jimmy Ellis had emerged as the WBA champion. In February of 1970 Frazier stopped the courageous Ellis to become the undisputed heavyweight champion, BUT...Muhammad Ali was coming out of exile. For Frazier to be regarded as the true champion, he had to defeat Ali. The table was now set for the "showdown" between Ali and Frazier.

After Joe Frazier defeated Muhammad Ali in their March 8, 1971, classic, in my eyes he was never the same. He had future moments, the win over Quarry, the "Thrilla in Manila", but for all intents and purposes, Joe left his soul in that Madison Square Garden ring. I have followed boxing for over forty years. In that time I have seen so many game warriors. I've seen men die in the ring, become disabled or suffer post career dementia.

For all the horrible things I've seen, one fight will always stand out for me. The first bout between Frazier and Ali was the Fight of the Century. Please have no doubt about it. In that fight I have never seen a boxer with such a will to win then Joe Frazier had that night. He was NOT going to be denied. Ali could have had a tire iron and a billy club in the ring with him that night, and he still would have lost. That night Joe Frazier could have held his own with any heavyweight that ever lived. On that glorious evening Joe Frazier was GREAT! That is how I'll always remember Joe Frazier.